hope & freedom

for Sexual Addicts
and Their Partners

Milton S. Magness, D.Min.

Gentle Path
P R E S S

Carefree, Arizona

Gentle Path Press
PO Box 3172
Carefree, Arizona 85377

www.gentlepath.com

Copyright © 2009 by Gentle Path Press

First Edition: August 2009

For more information regarding our publications,
please contact Gentle Path Press at
1-800-708-1796 (toll-free U.S. only).

Book edited by Greg Ottersbach and Marianne Harkin
Book designed by Serena Castillo

ISBN : 0-9774400-5-2

To my wife, Kathie,
who has always believed in me

Contents

Preface

This is a book about hope and ultimately, freedom. Compulsive sexual behavior, or sexual addiction, is often difficult to face. It results in countless negative consequences and hurts many people. Marriages and careers are destroyed by sexual addiction.

This is a book about hope because sexual addiction is treatable. Through hard work and a rigorous recovery program, it is possible for sexual addicts to stop their destructive behavior forever and for marriages and relationships to be restored. The recovery road is long and difficult and also very rewarding.

Whether you are a sexual addict, or the person you love is a sexual addict, you can find help within this book.

Recovery is a complete restoration of your spouse or partner's integrity and the reestablishment of trust in your relationship.

I engage in psychotherapy with sexual addicts and their spouses and loved ones because I see lives and relationships transformed daily. Some consider recovery to be the result of hard work alone, but I see it as a miracle; and I see miracles every day. Individuals once powerless to resist destructive behaviors overcome them, never to return. Marriages and other relationships on the brink of divorce or dissolution can be restored with trust reestablished.

If you are a sexual addict, or have a crisis caused by your partner's compulsive sexual behavior, this book is for you.

The goal is to bring you a message of hope and a way to achieve freedom, honesty and renewed trust in yourself and with the person you love.

Numerous sexual addicts who thought they could not stop have made a permanent break with compulsive sexual behavior. Many marriages once doomed for divorce have been resurrected and restored.

Recovery is not something one has to do but something one gets to do! If you can make a mental shift as you read this book, and see recovery as a gift instead of a penalty for bad behavior, you will be in a position to make extraordinary gains in your personal life. Recovery is a gift that comes from hard work to replace dysfunctional thoughts and behaviors. It leads to building a foundation to restore trust and leads to freedom from all compulsive sexual behavior and restores badly damaged relationships.

This book is addressed to sexual addicts and partners. While a larger percentage of men are sexual addicts, women also fall victim to addiction. Access to the Internet in particular has made it easy for women to engage in acting-out behaviors that would not have been as effortless in the past. It is unfair to address only male sexual addicts and fail to address female addicts. This book pertains to both genders.

Intimate long-term relationships in the United States are being redefined in ways others than traditional marriage. This book addresses any couples wanting to overcome sexual addiction for themselves or the person they love. In these pages, all relationships are perceived as affective relationships where trust and honesty are necessary for its survival.

The term used often by my colleagues is sex addict. In this book I have chosen to use the term sexual addict to soften the stigma often associated with the term sex addict.

Regardless of the term used, the condition is highly destructive to the individual who suffers with it as well as to those sharing the relationship. If you follow the steps described in this book, you will find freedom from addiction. A Chinese adage states, the hardest part of any journey is the first step. You have already began that journey by picking up this book.

Continue reading and I promise your life will change.

Acknowledgments

There are several people who have had a significant impact on my life as I founded Hope & Freedom Counseling Services and as I wrote this book. I would like to thank Dr. Patrick Carnes for developing the treatment model for sexual addiction. Your mentoring and friendship have meant more than you know.

Dr. Ralph Earle and Dr. Marcus Earle from Psychological Counseling Services in Scottsdale, Arizona have always been most gracious with their encouragement. I owe much of what Hope & Freedom has become to ideas I have borrowed from you.

I also wish to thank the many gifted colleagues who have made an impact on my life, including Adam Mason, Greg Curnutte, Enie Bourland, Doug Sorensen, Cara Weed, Jerry Goodman, Enod Gray, Dr. Barbara Levinson, Marsha Means, and Joni Ogle.

Finally, I wish to thank the many men and women who have come to Hope & Freedom. It has been a privilege to be a part of your journey.

Chapter 1

Sexual Addiction in America

Sexual addiction is a growing menace that threatens all strata of our society. Former presidents, governors, senators, leading actors, senior executives and other high-profile people have been disgraced when they admitted they were involved in some secret sexual behavior. Ministers, priests, doctors, lawyers, teachers, and community leaders have seen their careers cut short when they were caught in compromising sexual behaviors. Millions of marriages and relationships have been ruined or ended. Numerous reputations have been sacrificed on the altar of compulsive sexual behavior. Because certain sexual behavior is illegal, many have been sent to prison. Some have taken their own lives, rather than face the embarrassment of prosecution. Although not as well-known as other forms of addiction, such as alcohol, drugs and gambling, sexual addiction is responsible for the waste of billions of dollars annually. Worldwide revenue from pornography exceeds $100 billion a year.[1] Since 1997 pornography has had a steady annual growth rate of 40 percent[2] and the rate is increasing. There are other costs that figure in to the cost of sexual addiction. There are multiple lawsuits against the Catholic Church for sexual abuse of minors. The church has spent more than $2.6 billion in settlement costs and related expenses since 1950.[3] There are more than 12 million people exploited by trafficking in the sex trade.[4] Annual costs of medical treatment for sexually transmitted diseases in the U. S. exceeds $15.3 billion.[5]

Rafael's Story

Rafael was often told that he was attractive. When single he was always able to get dates and his pick of cute women. He has been in a committed relationship for two years. Fourteen months ago, he drove past a lovely young woman and offered her a ride. She asked him if he would like a date. He found out her idea of a "date" was that she was willing to be sexual with him as long as he was willing to give her shopping money. That was his first experience with a prostitute. He started picking up prostitutes in city locations frequented by them. He fancied himself a negotiator and would often spend the entire day propositioning them for sex acts and trying to see how cheaply he could make the deal. His behavior often put him at risk because these areas of his city were also drug infested and had a high incidence of violent crime.

I have spent years treating sexual addicts like Rafael, and encounter individuals from every walk of life, educational background and social standing. While every individual is unique the common denominator is overwhelming despair from being unable to control one's addiction or the sadness of seeing one's spouse or partner in the throes of addiction.

People Reaching for Help

I have pages of heart wrenching emails from people reaching out for help. To quote anonymously from a sample of the pleas:

From a woman, "Sexual addiction is ruining my life and I need your help. Sometimes I'll go out and pick up a guy, have sex with him, then go home to have sex with my husband … all in the same evening. I have been known to fly across the country to have sex with people I haven't even met face to face. I have had sex with my therapist, my doctor, my dentist, and even my brother. The list is endless. Please help me."

From a man, "I am 100 percent certain that I am a sex addict and feel I need immediate help as I feel it is ruining my life. It is very hard for me to concentrate on anything other than sex."

A wife's heartfelt concern, "Please tell me where I could get help for my husband. He is a sex addict. We have three beautiful children. I recently discovered a secret phone with the phone numbers of many different women and condoms with it. Please help me."

A worried father, "I have a son who began watching hardcore pornography clips on the Internet about two years ago. I am concerned that he will become an addict."

No profession is spared from sexual addiction: "I am an ordained minister and married with two children. For years I have struggled with homosexual attraction. I am attracted to my wife physically and sexually, and yet at the same time I find myself fighting attraction to men. Although I struggle with addiction to gay pornography and sex toys, I feel sick whenever I give into temptation. I cannot stop."

Sexual addiction manifests itself in an extensive variety of behavior or acting out which not limited to using pornography. One man wrote: "I am fighting this sexual addiction of dressing up and wanting to escalate my fantasies. My wife and children have no clue about what has been consuming me."

The addict's pain is always palpable: "I'm a long time sex-pornography addict. I've been to counselors piled on top of more counselors. This very day, I've hit bad websites and acted-out. I've been married to an angel for 11 years. It hurts. I'd be lying if I said it didn't."

Sometimes help comes too late, "My wife is planning to leave me because I can't stop looking at porn. I spend a lot of time on the computer looking at porn. It is constantly in the way of my relationship with my wife, and I'm going to lose her."

The son of a doctor wrote, "My father was caught with [explicit] pictures of his patients and is facing criminal charges. He and my mom need immediate counseling to help in this crisis."

One letter states the problem as a desire to be free from addiction, yet denies the addiction: "I have lost my wife and home, can't keep a job. I deny I have a problem, but yet my life is so out of control and stays that way. Why is that and what should I do?"

Palmer's Story

Travel was a way of life for Palmer. While out-of-town, his acting out was viewing Internet pornography and pay-per-view adult movies he could access from the hotels. He had been sober on an off for three years. Palmer attended meetings and even had a sponsor but felt he was not like other sex addicts because his acting out had consisted primarily of Internet pornography and compulsive masturbation.

He had just gone to his favorite acting-out website when someone knocked on the door. Opening the door just a crack, a hotel maid asked if she could put fresh towels in the bathroom. When she saw what he had been doing she propositioned him to have sex in his room. He was initially shocked and thought about telling management. The idea excited him and he had sex with the same maid and paid her for her services.

That was the beginning of a pattern for Palmer of checking in to hotels and making leading comments to hotel maids to see if he could find one willing to have sex with him. Sometimes he was successful but most of the time he was not. He felt this was a low risk behavior because even if he was turned down he doubted that he would be reported. He believed that people in low wage jobs would be reluctant to report something that could cost them their job.

As his courage grew, even when not traveling, he used the same technique of preying on unsuspecting women he thought would be vulnerable because of their low wages. He would especially target women working in parking booths at airports and cashiers at grocery stores. Sometimes he scored. Sometimes he struck out. He was always on the hunt. The pursuit consumed him.

Sexual Addiction

Such cases are not isolated examples of sexual addiction, Patrick Carnes, Ph.D., a forerunner in the initial identification and treatment of sexual addiction in his 1983 premier work on sexual addiction, *Out of the Shadows*, concluded that about 8 percent of men and about 5 percent of women in the United States are sexually addicted. The number has passed 15 million.[6] To revive a cliché, this is the tip of the iceberg. What lies below the surface is a terrifying image of unchecked sexual impulses impacting the morals of society.

Chapter 2

Hierarchy of Sexual Addiction

Benjamin's Story

Benjamin and his wife had been married three years when he told her that he had always had a fantasy of watching her have sex with another man. She had a visceral reaction to his fantasy and told him that would never happen. From time to time he reminded her of his fantasy and then asked if she would be willing to at least participate in the fantasy by saying shocking things to him while they were having sex. Benjamin continued to manipulate her and ask her to tell him how much she wanted to fulfill his fantasy.

While on a romantic weekend getaway, Benjamin convinced her to participate in a couple's erotic massage in their hotel room. Prior to the massage they were drinking heavily. She did not know that Benjamin had already told the man who was coming to do the massage that he wanted him to have sex with his wife. In her drunken state and with the pressure from Benjamin and the other man, she relented and had intercourse with this man while her husband watched. The next day she was devastated by what she had done. She knew her husband had taken advantage of her. She was angry that her husband thought so little of her that he violated clear boundaries that she had set.

Several weeks later Benjamin was shocked when he was served with divorce papers. He had no idea that his wife would react so badly to what he thought was a natural extension of his fantasy. Benjamin has started seeing a therapist and is attending 12-step meetings in an effort to save his marriage, which may not be salvageable. The fact that he is now in recovery is a positive step in the right direction. But for Benjamin to be truly successful in recovery long term, he must make a mental shift and do recovery work because it is something that he needs to do for himself, regardless of what happens in his relationship.

Although sexual addiction is not presently included in the Diagnostic and Statistical Manual of Mental Disorders (DSM-IV), the reference manual for all mental disorders, there is no professional denial of how its symptoms are comparable to other addictions. As does alcohol for the alcoholic, it offers a quick mood change, works every time and the user loses control over compulsive behavior. Like alcoholics, sexual addicts construct their lives around the need for their drug: sex. With alcoholics, there are undeniable signs of abuse and immediate penalties, such as arrest for DUI or public drunkenness. Alcoholism is a more socially overt addiction in terms of availability in public establishments such as bars and stores. Drugs, either illegal or abused prescriptions, are more clandestine in terms of purchase and use. They immediately betray the addict who gets high. For addicts, the hangover or come-down aftereffects are physical.

Sexual addiction is more subtle in how it can be experienced and maintained. Sexual addiction may take many forms. Compulsive masturbation, viewing pornography, or being sexual with other people. Others may express their sexual addiction by becoming involved in illegal activities, such as solicitation of prostitution, exhibitionism, or voyeurism. The common denominator is that all sexual addicts feel driven to participate in their sexual behavior regardless of the risk and no matter the consequences. "

The Society for the Advancement of Sexual Health defines several recurring components of sexual addiction: "Compulsivity, a loss of the ability to choose freely whether to stop or to continue; continuation of the behavior despite adverse consequences, such as loss of health, marriage, or freedom, and obsession with the activity."[7] Unlike chemical addiction, which is limited to alcoholic beverages, or a choice of narcotics, sexual addiction is not limited in the way it may be acted out, and can even occur entirely within the imagination, such as thinking about women in swimming suits at a beach, or fantasizing a sexual scene while driving. As undetectable as are some forms of imagined sexual addiction, the most common visible forms are recognizable:

- Sexual promiscuity
- Pornography
- Sexually oriented businesses; massage parlors, gentleman's clubs
- Prostitution
- Escort services
- Exhibitionism
- Voyeurism
- Cross-dressing

The term "sexual addiction" is often misunderstood. For some, realizing there is a name for out-of-control sexual behavior is a relief. It helps explain why a person will continue behavior knowing the risk to his or her relationship, health, job/career or freedom. For others, the term feels like a label charged with negative implications without hope.

Aaron's Story

Aaron would not consider living an openly gay lifestyle because it conflicted with his conservative religious beliefs. He always suspected that he was gay but has never been able to reconcile his beliefs with his actions. He has been successful hiding his sexual behavior from everyone he knows.

As far as any of his friends know, he is a single man who occasionally has dates with women but prefers to remain single. His friends do not know is that Aaron has engaged in secret sexual rendezvous with men for many years. Most consist of anonymous encounters with strangers. He struggles with guilt over his sexual behavior but feels powerless to stop.

Gay or straight, male or female, sexual addiction is an equal opportunity addiction and does not discriminate. Although sexual addiction is not considered a diagnosable disorder by some mental health professionals, for the person who suffers from it or is in a relationship with someone having the addiction, there is no question that it is a legitimate affliction. If you prefer the term hyper-sexuality, or sexual compulsivity disorder, then mentally insert your term each time you see the term sexual addiction in this book. From my clinical experience I believe sexual addiction is a valid disorder affecting many.

William's Story

William was in his second year of medical school when he found a sex chat room while looking for something to break the monotony of studying. To his surprise, he found people who were very open about their sexual desires and behaviors. To say that he was captivated by what he saw would be an understatement. After a few hours of what William thought was a harmless diversion, he went back to his studies.

The next night he was back in the chat room and ended up spending much more time than he intended. Short on sleep, he went to class the next day but fell more behind than ever. In the evening he sought comfort in various chat rooms. Somehow he managed to successfully complete the school year but realized that his cybersex behaviors were getting out of hand.

William tried to stop but found himself back in the chat rooms after a hiatus of only a few days. The third year of medical school was the most challenging yet. Rather than being able to meet the challenge he retreated into the comfortable and predictable cybersex behavior that made him forget the pressure of school for hours. Each day he would look forward to the end of his classes when he was able to escape into his fantasy world. To his dismay, William fell hopelessly behind and was unable to get current on his assignments. Even after being shown significant leniency by his professors, he knew he would not be able to catch up. Finally the dean asked him to resign from school and save himself the embarrassment of flunking out. How could this happen? His grades in high school and college were always at the top of the class. He had one of the highest scores ever on his entrance exam. The only thing that explains William's dramatic fall was that he was firmly in the clutches of sexual addiction.

At least one in twenty people meet the criteria for addiction. It could be as high as one in ten. Using the more conservative figure means that there are as many sexual addicts in the United States as there are people with bipolar disorder, obsessive compulsive disorder, panic disorder, and schizophrenia combined! Put another way, there are as many sexual addicts in the United States as people living in New York, Chicago, Los Angeles, Houston, and Boston combined!

Sexual addiction is not rare, in spite of the fact that many people have never heard the term. A casual review of today's media validates the extent of disruptive and destructive compulsive sexual behavior going on daily. Much of what passes for entertainment on TV, movies, or comedy clubs is thinly veiled sexual addiction. Worse is when sexual addiction is portrayed as humorous. One may wonder if there would be much left to entertain people if innuendo or explicit content about compulsive sexual behavior were removed from our entertainment.

Brian's Story

Brian has a secret he has never told anyone. He has a fetish with women's panties. It began when he was thirteen. He found a pair of his older sister's panties in the bathroom. He was fascinated by the material and the construction of the underwear so different from his briefs. He kept the panties in his room and would sometimes wear them while he masturbated. As he grew older he would look for opportunities to steal underwear from his sister's friends. When he would have sleep overs at his friends' houses, he would go through drawers of their sisters and mothers as well as the dirty clothes hamper, adding to his panty collection.

Over the years he has spent a lot of time cruising laundry rooms in apartment complexes looking for unattended dryers that may contain underwear. He has often bought lingerie which he asks his sexual partners to wear. While they usually accommodate his requests, some are irritated because he seems more interested in their underwear than their bodies. A couple of his partners have caught him trying to steal their underwear and once he was chased out of a laundromat by a guard that had been alerted to his odd behavior. In spite of the potential consequences he does not believe it is possible for him to stop stealing panties. Although he sometimes purchases underwear, he gets a higher sexual arousal from stealing them.

Compulsive Sexual Behaviors

A variety of problematic sexual behaviors may be present in sexual addicts. There are several hundred identified compulsive sexual behaviors. This list names a few:

- Compulsive masturbation, sometimes to the point of injury
- Renting or purchasing pornography photographs, movies, games, and/or magazines
- Engaging in sexual emails, chat rooms, or other sexual behavior on the Internet
- Engaging in phone sex
- Frequenting sexually oriented businesses (such as strip clubs, sexual massage parlors modeling studios, bath houses, and adult bookstores or arcades)
- Having sex with prostitutes
- Engaging in sex in exchange for payment
- Carrying on multiple relationships at once
- Having anonymous sex
- Engaging in sadomasochistic or "pain exchange" sex
- Using drugs or alcohol to heighten sexual euphoria
- Exhibitionism
- Voyeurism

- Professional boundary violations (as with physicians, attorneys, therapists, and clergy)
- Indecent phone calls
- Touching people in a sexual manner without their permission, which is known as frotteurism

While a higher percentage of men traditionally act out these forms of behavior, women are entering more into arenas of sexual addiction. The presence of one or several sexual behaviors is not proof that a person is a sexual addict. Certainly, sexual behaviors outside of a marriage or relationship predicated on monogamy damages the relationship. The presence of certain behaviors is not an indication that a person is a sexual addict. A number of factors must be considered before an individual can be diagnosed as a sexual addict.

Sexual addiction is a way some people medicate their feelings and cope with stress. As with drugs that are often abused for the same purposes, sex is effective in temporarily relieving pain. Subsequent uses of sex as self-administered medication for stress and loneliness requires more frequent sexual behavior or perhaps even more risky behavior to achieve the same relief as before.

Sexual addicts may find themselves unable to control, their behavior. They may use inordinate amounts of time to pursue their addiction. Trying to control their behavior, they make promises to themselves, to those they love, even make vows to God that they will stop. But they are unable to stop.

Among some spiritual people, sexual addiction may be an effort to fill a void in their lives that only God, or a higher spiritual force, or a sense of meaning to life, can fill. Even religious persons having a personal relationship with God may use sex to give their lives meaning. With each sexual encounter they find temporary relief for loneliness or low self-esteem. But they find that their "fix" lasts for increasingly shorter durations each time, necessitating an escalation in addictive behavior. A typical course of sexual addiction includes an escalation of behaviors and the development of an increasing tolerance as a requirement for more sex or more extreme sexual behavior to be satisfied.

Sexual addicts may isolate themselves from others, sometimes to the point of having little or no contact with people. They may find their primary sexual outlet with pornography or cybersex activities and not want to risk rejection that could come from moving from the omnipotent power in a virtual landscape, to a world of living human beings with their own emotional needs.

It is common for sexual addicts to feel that their lives are out of control. They may experience a loss of time where they find many hours passing during their acting out but feel that only a few minutes have passed. Sexual addicts may use dishonesty to cover activities. Persons who are otherwise uncompromisingly honest may engage in blatant fabrications, lies, and contrived excuses to cover their sexual behavior as well as time and money expended in their sexual pursuits.

Most surprising is that as in drug addiction, some sexual addicts suffer withdrawal symptoms if they are unable to act out. Symptoms may include restlessness, irritability, insomnia, and such a preoccupation with sex that they are unable to function at their job or with their families.

The presence of several of these symptoms may be an indication that a person is a sexual addict. For a more accurate diagnosis, one should seek a psychotherapist skilled in diagnosing and treating sexual addiction, or contact any of the organizations dealing with sexual addiction found in the reference section of this book.

In cases where a companion has admitted to being a sexual addict but has not explained the reason for the behavior, the partner is left to wonder what sexual acting-act is taking place when they are not together. They may wonder what else their partner is doing. The descriptions of sexual addiction in this book are intended to enlighten and not to be offensive. They help you understand sexual behaviors often sought by sexual addicts.

This book does provide a detailed discussion about sexual behaviors, but also covers of more common ways sexual addiction manifests itself and how it can be identified.

Robbie's Story

Robbie manages a successful hedge fund. He is always under pressure to perform and produce results for his clients. For a change of pace during the day, he will occasionally turn to the Internet and spend a few minutes acting out. These forays into fantasy have lately occupied more of his time. He first discovered virtual 3-D websites a couple of years ago. Robbie loved to go to those sites, and adopt a fictional identity and follow his made up character through the normal routines of life.

Gradually, he moved from the ordinary routines of life to developing elaborate fictional characters, or avatars, to allow him to live out his sexual fantasies online. At first he would pretend to be the man he thought women would like. He then had fantasy sex with them. Robbie soon found more excitement from becoming the object of his affection. Since his ideal sex partners are twenty-four year old petite blonds, he decided to take on the role of various young women and then find sexual fulfillment vicariously through them.

To make his avatar more convincing, Robbie would spend many hours each week creating the perfect profile. He would scour various pornography sites and social networking sites for photos of young women that fit his profile. To make the most credible profiles, he felt he needed not only nude photos of young women but also photos of them going through daily life, visiting with family and friends. There were weeks that Robbie spent more hours developing elaborate profiles than working at his job. After spending a few hours acting out with each avatar he created, he would start developing a new character that would be his obsession for the following week.

As the result of acting out, Robbie lost key clients and his hedge fund is performing well below the market. With this increased pressure to perform at a higher level, he turned more frequently to his virtual world which resulted in even poorer performance. Robbie knows he has to stop his acting out completely or he will destroy his business. However, he is unable to stop his self-destructive behavior.

New Dangers of Addictive Anonymity

Sadly, advances in technology have made it easy for sexual addicts to act out their fantasies with less chance of discovery. Virtual websites such as Second Life and Ever Quest allow members to engage virtually in many forms of sexual behavior with others, while remaining anonymous, even to the extent of changing sexes. Acting-out is achieved through an avatar.

The virtual world creates temptation for sexual addicts and pain for their real world partners. Every second $3,075.64 is being spent on pornography, 28,258 internet users are viewing pornography, and 372 internet users are typing adult search terms into search engines.[8] On the Internet anything goes, and sexual addicts can act out with ease, even visiting many sexual sites at not charge. As long as they can conceal their activities from spouses, employers or peers, addiction is fostered. When they are caught, lives and relationships may be destroyed.

Individuals may be engaging in sexually addictive behavior online, thinking that because they are not in direct contact with others, there is no danger to them or their partner. They are mistaken. Sexual addiction leads to emotional distance from loved ones and lying and deceit to conceal the addiction. Shame and guilt are constant emotions. The impact goes beyond acting out in private. The cost to employers from workers using 25 percent or more of company time to visit pornographic websites is substantial. But the greatest damage addicts do is to themselves by hiding their addiction until it overtakes their life.

No technological advance has done more to facilitate sexual addiction than the Internet. It provides multiple opportunities to act out sexually and is a powerful accelerant to sexual addiction.

The late Dr. Al Cooper, a researcher at Stanford University, stated that there are people who are sexual addicts today that would never have been addicted without the Internet. Access of the Internet makes things available at home that were previously only available in seedy adult entertainment establishments.

Dr. Cooper explained the addictive power of the Internet in what he called the *Triple A Engine*. The Internet is *Available*, anyone can access it from home or computer anywhere in the world. It is *Affordable*, for little cost or in many cases free, and pornographic images can be viewed, catalogued, and saved for additional viewing later. Many sexual addicts want to make clear that they "never paid for any Internet pornography" as if they are less of a sexual addict because they did not spend money for their pornography. Finally, it is *Anonymous*, rather than having to enter an adult establishment and risk being recognized by one's neighbors, it is possible to peruse the Internet in relative anonymity.[9]

A primary activity of sexual addicts on the Internet is viewing pornography. These images may be photos, movies, or cartoons. Few are as relatively tame as the airbrushed photos associated with Playboy or Playgirl magazines. Rather, the pornography of the Internet is more graphic, hard core, and provides a neurochemical release of such magnitude that it is often instantly addicting to the viewer. Things that many people never dreamed of are depicted with such detail that nothing is left to the imagination.

Internet pornography ranges from explicit photos or movies of people having sex, and sexual acts involving heterosexual and homosexual sex, sex in single and group situations, sex involving foreign objects, sex with animals, and sex with children. Anything that a person can possibly imagine can be found on the Internet.

While there are millions of free pornographic images on the Internet, however, pornographers are in business to make money. They sell subscriptions to their sites for one-time viewing where subscribers are allowed to return to the site at will without paying additional fees. Some websites take credit card or Pay Pal charges which often show up on one's bill as a seemingly innocuous charge.

Often companies are identified by initials or are disguised to resemble legitimate businesses. Charges range from $10 to $50 or more. The charges may be one-time events or set up to automatically charge the card as a monthly subscription. While subscription fees are common, paid advertising and selling link exchanges accounts for a large percentage of their revenues as well.

This industry is so lucrative and growing so rapidly that any figures describing its size are out of date before they are printed. Another of addictive sexual behavior involving the Internet is sexually explicit chat. Many services provide "adult chat rooms" that are specific to a person's individual proclivity. The categories will include things like "Married but Looking," "Barely Legal," "Steamy Seniors," or other provocative and often pornographic titles

Jackie's Story

Jackie has been married to the same man for almost 20 years. A few years ago she believed that she may have missed something in life because she did not have any of the excitement that she craved. She started entertaining herself by going to chat rooms that were advertised for people who were "married but looking." Jackie had no intention of ever doing more than talking to the men she met online.

In the chat rooms she could portray herself as the person that she secretly wanted to be. And to her surprise, there were many men that wanted to talk with her and most suggested that they meet in person. Not wanting to be physically unfaithful to her husband she successfully deflected all of the requests for face-to-face meetings. At least she deflected them until she decided to meet someone who was insistent that she reminded him of his old high school girlfriend.

Before long, she was regularly engaging in secret meetings with men that she would first contact in the chat rooms and then meet at a secret location. What started as a seemingly harmless diversion ended up a full blown sexual addiction and divorce.

Chat Rooms

Chat rooms provide an open forum for people to meet and post electronic messages that can be seen by others in the "room." Each person in the room uses an identifier known as a "handle" rather than his or her real name. In the sexual chat rooms it is common to see handles like "Hot to Trot in Tulsa," or "Sexy and Ready in Seattle." If participants want, they have the option of leaving the open chat room and go to a "private room" where they can have personal sexual conversations that may result in a face-to-face encounter.

Another area of acting out on the Internet involves reading or writing sexual fantasies. There are countless sites that contain graphic sexual fantasies. Some allow stories to be downloaded and others for posting fantasies or for swapping stories. Worldwide more than 75 million people visit pornographic websites monthly.[10] However, this number is deceptively low. There is also a high percentage of peer-to-peer traffic offering pornographic materials. Peer-to-peer traffic is not captured as visits to pornographic websites.

In addition, consider the intrusiveness of pornography in the pop-ups and spam emails reaching people are innocently working on their computers. The pornography industry grabs tens of thousands of expired URLs each month and redirects people to active pornography sites. This so-called "porn-napping," has been experienced by most Internet users looking for a legitimate site and finding a pornography site.

Adults are not the only ones impacted by Internet pornography. The average age of first exposure to Internet pornography is eleven. The newest practice among teens is the sending text messages with attachments of nude or semi-nude photos of themselves to friends, known as "sexting". An alarming 20 percent of teens admit that they have been engaged in x-rated text messaging.[11]

Phone Sex

Phone sex lines predate the Internet. They are responsible for 976 and 900 phone numbers that automatically add toll charges to the phone bill of the caller.

Although overt phone sex is illegal, loopholes allow the purveyors of the services to operate openly with little fear of prosecution. Charges for services range from a few cents to several dollars per minute. The typical use of phone sex is for the caller to tell his or her fantasy to the listener and then have the listener "talk dirty" while the caller masturbates. These numbers are frequently advertised in urban newspapers.

A New Spin on Voyeurism and Exhibitionism

Haden's Story
Haden was intrigued with miniature video cameras advertised online. He bought one, telling himself that he was going to use it for security in his home. Instead he installed it in his bathroom so he could secretly view overnight guests' behaviors. He then saved the videos on his computer.

After several months of secretly recording videos of his friends, his daughter spotted something shiny in the vent in the bathroom. She told her mother who discovered the camera. Incensed by what she found, she searched her husband's computer and found some of the videos. She took the computer to the police. After finding images of several young girls on his computer, Haden was arrested for possession of child pornography. He is awaiting trial.

The traditional image of a voyeur is the so-called "peeping tom" who lurks outside of bedroom windows hoping to see something tantalizing. However consider what happened to this woman at a well-known hotel in a large city.

Veronica's Story
Veronica was in town for a business meeting. Following her morning routine, she went out for an early three mile run and returned to her

room to get ready for her meeting. Instead of turning on the light switch by the door of her darkened room, she walked across the room to turn on a lamp. Her eye was caught a small beam of light on the mirror above the sink. She inspected the light closer and found that it was coming from behind the mirror. Putting her eye close to the mirror Veronica could tell that the backing had been scraped away from the mirror allowing her to see into a room behind the mirror.

Frightened by what she had found, she called the local police and told a detective what she discovered. The detective returned with her to the room and removed the mirror. A hole was revealed that led to a utility area that ran the entire length of the floor between adjacent rooms.

Hotel management was summoned to access the utility area, which revealed that every room had a small peephole allowing unrestricted viewing of the room. In ensuing investigation a maintenance man confessed that he had a several webcams he set up in the space. He video taped people in their rooms and also spent hours watching. While claiming this was his first such encounter, he revealed that when he was a child he used to watch his siblings through the bathroom door keyhole.

While the incident may be an anomaly, it points out that we must get beyond traditional stereotypes of sexual acting out. With the advent of the Internet and inexpensive webcams, both voyeurism and exhibitionism have been greatly facilitated.

Misuse of webcams is common. When a webcam is installed, the software often allows the user to alert others online that a webcam is in use and able to link the to other webcams. This should be of special concern to parents. Not only can children be targeted but they may be tempted to reenact juvenile "show me yours and I'll show you mine" games with strangers.

Traditional Sites of Acting Out:
Bookstores and Bathhouses

Hector's Story

Hector recalls the shame he felt when he would have to shower after gym class in school. He was sure his penis was much smaller than the other boys. When he heard about pumps that would enlarge his penis, he ordered one from an ad in a men's magazine. The device did not work so he searched for other devices. None of the devices worked but he got a degree of comfort believing that he was a "late bloomer." He thought that he was just a bit behind other boys and would catch up later.

By the time he got to college he realized that he would have to live with the body parts he was born with. But Hector was not able to get over his obsession with the size of his penis. While he believed that he was heterosexual, he began acting out with men in the backrooms of adult bookstores. Hector received affirmation from being with other men, especially when he realized that many of them were not put off by his small size. He has tried to stop his acting out with men, believing it was a bad habit that he can control. Hector has been unable to resist the urge to return to the same activities after making self promises that he will never repeat them.

Adult bookstores offer a variety of pornography and sometimes private booths where it is possible to view hard core pornographic movies. These booths are usually dark and used for anonymous sexual encounters, primarily for men for sex with other men. Some have "glory holes" in the wall of the adjoining booth that allows anonymous sex for the participants to engage in without having to see the other person or to interact in any other way. Such bookstores are often dangerous, but some men feel so drawn to them that they find it nearly impossible to go more than a few days without visiting one.

Taamir's Story

Taamir moved to Chicago from the Middle East when he was fifteen. Having spent the first years of his life in a closed country, he had never seen pornography. Shortly after arriving in America he discovered that he could access pornography from any computer.

He heard stories about what was available on the Internet but had never seen anything that was forbidden in his country. He was shocked with what he found on the Internet, but his shock soon turned to fascination. By the time he was twenty, he spent everyday either looking at pornography or trying to find someone who was willing to have sex. His meetings with acting out partners became more frequent. Eventually he discovered bathhouses and soon was engaging in high risk anonymous sexual behavior.

The bathhouses referred to here exist in many large American or European cities, especially those with a large gay population. They are places where men hang out to have sex with other men. Often the goal is to have sex with as many as possible.

Massage Parlors, Spas, Escort Services, and Related Businesses

Cole's Story

Cole's long-time partner, Sharon, experiences significant pain during intercourse. While she was working with her doctor to address her pain from a medical standpoint, Cole decided he would seek out the services of a massage parlor that offered a "happy ending" or would masturbate him for a "tip." He rationalized that he was not really cheating on his partner because he was not emotionally involved with anyone and had great love for Sharon. Besides, he was taking the pressure off of Sharon to satisfy him sexually while she addressed her physical problems.

Gradually, Cole's trips to massage parlors increased to multiple times per week. He was no longer content with the manual stimulation he received but found that, for a price, he could engage in any sexual act. He stopped the pretense that he was there for a massage and would just pay for sex.

Cole tried to stop acting out but felt compelled to return to massage parlors to satisfy his addiction to sex. Results from a blood test reported that he has a sexually transmitted disease. How is he going to explain this to Sharon?

Some massage parlors set up to offer sex to their patrons should not to be confused with legitimate massage therapists. Some "sexual" massage parlors are front for prostitution. They focus on selling sexual services and not on therapeutic massage. There are often signs for these, such as their location and how they market their services.

These "sexual" massage parlors operate many ways but in the end the client always pays someone to perform sex.

Modeling studios and lingerie studios are another disguise for brothels that can be found in many large cities. Some require their patrons pay a cover charge to enter and are allowed to watch women model various clothes or undergarments that they may want to purchase. These "studios" do not have anything to do with modeling clothing. They are others examples of houses of prostitution.

In some cities there are advertisements for photography studios. These supposedly allow photographers to find a model to pose nude. Some studios often rent cameras in case the customer does not have one, to give a greater appearance of legitimacy. But as with other sexual businesses, services offered behind closed doors provide more than just visual stimulation.

Escort services are plentiful and often operate rather openly. They are advertised widely on the Internet. Do not believe the claims that these are just services that provide dates or social companions for lonely people. This is prostitution any way you look at it. The "escorts" will pay a portion of their fee to their agency but will make their real money on "tips" which are actually payment for sexual services.

It is common to pay $1,000 or more for an "escort" and to develop such an addiction to this behavior that they may even become convinced that they are in love with an escort they meet. Such misplaced emotions evolve because some of the time the escort will not charge or because their encounters often include long periods of talk as well as sex.

An old German expression says, "Be a lamb and the wolf shall appear." The same caution holds for sexual addiction. Give in to your impulses and your addiction will talk hold.

Our permissive society requires strong individual discipline, especially when it comes to sexual responsibility. It is not just the danger of contracting or passing on HIV or STDs that makes promiscuity damaging; it is the effect it has on the spouse or partner when the sexual addict repeatedly and compulsively engages in self-indulgent forms of repetitious behavior, creating lies and spreading deceit to conceal the addiction.

Just as the alcoholic sometimes needs to "hit bottom" to realize the seriousness of the problem, so do many sexual addicts to experience a crisis. It could take exposure by a spouse, arrest by the police, termination by an employer, or shame being caught by family or friends, to realize being are at the mercy of the addiction.

Sexual Addiction of Physicians, Clergy, Senior Executives, and Celebrities

Sexual addicts who are physicians, clergy, senior executives and other high-salaried individuals or celebrities, have much in common. They may perceive themselves as different from "ordinary" people. They may believe they live by a different set of rules for the rest of society. How do they justify this double standard? Simply because of the power they wield in their positions, or the money they earn, which may be many times or more than "ordinary" people earn. All four groups have numerous experiences reinforcing the belief that they are not like ordinary people.

Physician Sexual Addicts

Ravi's Story

A successful physician, Ravi enjoyed the finer things in life, but he did not get nearly as much pleasure from possessing nice things as he did from pursuing sex. A strip club near his office offered a "businessman's special," which was a lunch buffet for two dollars and cover charge. Ravi developed the habit of eating at the club three days each week. He got to know the dancers by name and started dating one. He became interested in her when she told him she was working her way through medical school. In order for her to be able to go out on a date she needed him to cover the money she lost from tips by not working for the night. He was shocked to find out that she needed one thousand dollars to make up for lost tips. Their relationship developed with them having a "date" once or twice a week. He eventually realized that her story about attending medical school was a lie. Before getting into recovery, Ravi realized that the large amount of money he spent for the past year had been going primarily to his favorite dancer.

Society often places physicians on a pedestal. Many people are raised not to challenge anything a physician says or does. As well-educated experts on health, physicians are respected, even revered in some communities. They are used to getting great respect and perhaps even reverence.

In fairness to all physicians, it should be noted that only a few seek this kind of attention and adulation. In fact, most may go out of their way to present themselves as ordinary people who happen to be practicing the healing arts.

The hero worship prevails. Grateful patients and families of patients express their appreciation and tell physicians how they saved lives. They may hear things like, "You are the most gifted surgeon," or, "Without you, I wouldn't be alive," or "Our town is fortunate to have you practicing here." Sincere comments may add to a physician's belief that he or she is not like ordinary people.

Often self-justification is self reward with sexual behavior that appears to be innocuous. They may believe they need a reward for their long hours, unselfish devotion and humanitarian efforts, or because they are so intelligent. Physicians may not have many relationships with people outside of their work, leading them to live isolated lives.

Clergy Sexual Addicts

Keenan's Story

Keenan wanted to be a minister since he was a teen. He also struggled with pornography from the same time. He would never think of violating his professional standards by beginning a sexual relationship with someone in his congregation. Because of his stature in his denomination, he is highly sought as a conference speaker and has a heavy travel schedule. On every trip Keenan scours the yellow pages and free press newspapers for spas and massage parlors. He is usually successful finding someone willing to be sexual with him. While he feels guilty about his behavior, he reminds himself that he is helping many people through his ministry and that he is under extraordinary stress because of his busy schedule. He reasons that he deserves some relaxation and that his sexual behavior is not harming anyone.

Clergy often work long hours for little pay. They may find they are always giving of themselves and seldom receiving. And as they perform their duties, there are often people who will express their appreciation for many things a minister, priest, or rabbi does for them or their congregation. Clergy are used to positive feedback about their sermons. They may hear, "You're the best pastor we've ever had. God blessed us by sending you," or "No other rabbi has given so much of himself to the community."

Most clergy do not seek to be put on a pedestal and do not ask to be idolized. But with the continued praise, some clergy may believe that they deserve something extra for their efforts.

As with all sexual addicts, their acting out behavior may include a wide variety of sexual activities. Sadly, physician and clergy acting out may include professional boundary violations where they are involved sexually with patients, parishioners, or staff. Regardless of the behaviors involved, both physicians and clergy are often more isolated than other sexual addicts and may find it more difficult to seek help for fear of being discovered.

One only has to look at the on-going tragedy concerning the molestation of young boys by Catholic priests. The violation of trust is profound. In this situation, sexual addiction no longer affects one person and his spouse or companion; it is an on-going behavior destroying countless lives, of both the victims and the victimizers. One can see the terrible consequences of unchecked addiction, especially if it can be concealed behind a position of power or unquestioned authority. While sexual abuse of minors by priests have garnered most of the headlines, there are numerous instances of prominent ministers who have been accused of sexual improprieties.

Senior Executive Sexual Addicts

Omar's Story

Omar had been the chief operating officer of a major corporation for nearly ten years. He was known as a "player" by many of the employees and had several consensual sexual relationships with various employees. His last affair with an employee began similarly to the others. It consisted of business lunches out-of-town business trips used for sex. While he was not this person's direct supervisor, he knew he was jeopardizing his job by having sex with a subordinate.

Rumors began to circulate throughout the company while people speculated as to whether there was something more to his association with that particular employee than a work relationship. The employee was so embarrassed upon hearing the rumors that she went to the human resources department and confessed the relationship. She feared getting fired for sleeping with this executive. Instead, the company launched an internal investigation and then confronted Omar with the information. Omar reluctantly admitted that he had an affair with this person but pointed out that it had ended a month earlier, he never felt that it compromised his job.

He was dismissed by his company and was subsequently sued for sexual harassment. The six figure settlement was borne partly by his company but mostly by himself. Worst yet was that other companies in his industry that might have been the source of future employment blackballed him from any position in his industry.

Some executives, entrepreneurs, and highly compensated individuals may believe their wealth and success separates them from the rest of society. They may see their success as evidence that they are unlike ordinary people. Their ability to be innovative and successful by going against conventional wisdom may reinforce their belief that they are not subject to the rules and behavioral norms of the rest of society.

Because of financial resources, there is a higher incidence of paying for sex than with others. One has only to look at the fall from power of various industry leaders and politicians and to see all the characteristics of individuals perceiving themselves above the rules and beyond the laws of society. Sexual addicts who are senior executives may pay significant money for various sex partners. They may not see this as prostitution but rather believe they are just helping someone out by providing living expenses and gifts and very extravagant gifts to their paramour. The greater the power, the greater is the ability to rationalize one's abuse of power.

Renaldo's Story

Renaldo was a successful businessman who had built his company from scratch to a thriving business in thirty years. He always believed his wife took his success for granted and did not acknowledge how well he provided for her and their children. Renaldo wanted to be appreciated and praised for his financial success. He was drawn to websites that featured women who wanted to be taken care of financially.

After meeting one woman and, to use his words, "falling in lust with her," he agreed to provide her an apartment and a car. The apartment was less than a block from his office so he could slip over to see her during the day when he needed a break from the stress of work. After a few months, she left with the car he bought her and the many gifts as well as the cash he gave her.

Over several years, this scenario was repeated with multiple women, and each had a "phantom position" in his company and was on the company payroll, and had a car that was placed in her name. While Renaldo wanted to stop this cycle of dead-end relationships, he reasoned that he could afford it and he was not really harming anyone by his compulsive behavior.

Money and access are extremely empowering to the executive sexual addict who can escape detection for a long time with little repercussion. The wherewithal and significant amount of travel using hotels is extremely enabling. The sex trade that targets executives is found at all common business destinations: hotels, convention and conference centers; and is advertised and marketed with hand out flyers and explicit in-room advertisements. Even hotel concierges, if asked, often provide numbers and contacts to escorts and the local sex trade.

Celebrity Sexual Addicts

Andy's Story

Andy recalls the first time he looked at pornography when he found a stash of magazines in a vacant apartment near his home. From the first look he was hooked. He carefully guarded his treasure and hid it so that no one else could find it and take it from him. He began to sneak daily to this vacant apartment to look at the pictures. When he was not looking at the images he was fantasizing about them.

In high school, Andy's natural athletic ability earned him a place on the varsity squad in several sports. His success coupled with good looks, earned the attention of many girls. Throughout college he excelled with sports and became known as a womanizer, which continued into his professional life in sports. Andy moved from relationship to relationship with little more thought than he gave to changing sports cars: to have the newest and fastest.

As far as anyone knew, Andy was successful in every area of life. But he knew he was incapable of stopping his acting out on his own. He never built a lasting relationship with anyone and felt all alone. To make matters worse, he realized his fame worked against him. He knew that it was impossible to get help for his addiction which would expose his private life to the world on the network news.

Treatment

Treatment for those seeking anonymity is similar to that of other sexual addicts. Intensives are tailored especially for them to help them overcome the assumption they are not like other people.

There are locations offering 12-step meetings for professionals. Some have meetings only for clergy and others open only to physicians. These are helpful because members of these groups often face a challenge to attend 12-step meetings if they believe they are in a different class. Sexual addiction is the great leveler. Ironically, the more power and money that goes into maintaining the addiction, the greater is the fall. Hitting bottom is the moment when the addict realizes he either must seek immediate help or lose everything. Many executives or celebrity addicts do not heed the message of hitting bottom because they believe they are safe at the top. Then they fall farther when they are finally exposed.

Chapter 3

Addressing the Sexual Addict

Stuart's Story

Stuart has been dressing up like a woman for years. Each time he does, he tries to lure men into sexual relationships where he performs sexual favors on them but goes no further so that he would not to be discovered to be a man. He doesn't recall the first time but remembers when he found a discarded pair of his mother's pantyhose when he was about seven or eight. He tried them on to see what he looked like. When he was a teen, Stuart was dressing up in his mother's clothes any time that she was away. He would walk around town and was thrilled when men gave him attention.

Stuart felt most free to act out when he traveled for out-of-town on business. He frequently shipped company supplies ahead in preparation for a business meeting, and would often pack his dress up clothes with the company supplies. The boxes were shipped to his hotel with a notation that they were only to be opened by him. This allowed him to pack a carryon piece of luggage and reduced the possibility that his wife would discover his secret behavior.

On one trip his flight was delayed by weather causing him to arrive late. What he did not know was that his boss arrived earlier than scheduled. His boss retrieved the supply box from the hotel and unpacked it to prepare for the meeting. Imagine his surprise when he found women's clothes in the company box, complete with a photo of Stuart in drag! The next week Stuart looked for treatment for his sexual addiction.

The Crisis

The crisis that brought you to recovery is the proverbial blessing in disguise. The crisis may be the threat or loss of relationship, job, heath, or freedom. As painful as it is, if crisis leads you into recovery, it can be the best thing that ever happened to you.

I have heard confessions of years of acting out and also have heard individuals reveal that their acting out began only recently. Women have said they turned on their computer found a secret email their spouse wrote to a lover. A man finished a cell phone conversation with his wife and then propositioned a prostitute, that later learned his spouse overheard the entire episode because he forgot to press "end" to finish the phone call. One woman became addicted to compulsive sexual behavior concealed behind the fantasy of an avatar on the Internet site, Second Life.

Often the crisis is difficult to face. But if crisis leads to recovery and changes how you live, it can be a turning point for you to move forward.

If you are reading this book, you know there is no longer a chance for things remaining the same. Even the crises of losing a job or being arrested may be seen as a gift because it is the beginning of the recovery road. I ask that you try your very best to adhere to the message and the methods of hope and freedom described in this book for you and your partner.

Hope and Freedom for Both of You

For your relationship to be restored, you, the sexual addict, and your partner must ultimately commit to the difficult but rewarding journey called recovery. The paths each of you takes may be different but have the same goal.

Though it may seem unfair, your partner will need to be involved in their own recovery, even though you have the addiction. Your addiction has greatly impacted the person you love.

Your acting out can come to an end. This may seem unachievable to you. You may have tried numerous "cures" throughout the years and believe that you are beyond help.

You must not give up hope that your acting out can come to an end and the hope that you can finally commit to being faithful to your partner. All sexual addicts hope to become truly content and not go outside the boundaries of their marriages and loving relationships.

This may seem like the impossible dream, but I have seen the dream come true many times.

- Recovery means an end to wanderlust.
- Recovery means the end to concealment and deceit.
- Recovery means hope for you to be a person of integrity.
- There is no time but Now and there is no place but Here

As a great rabbi of the 13th Century wrote, "If I am not for myself, who is? If I am only for myself, what am I? If not now, when?"

Immediate Steps toward Hope & Freedom

End problematic relationships. The first action for sexual addicts is to terminate all contact with acting-out partners. This means contacting each of them and explicitly stating that the relationship is over. This contact should be done under supervision of a trusted friend or therapist.

Change cell phone number and email address. These actions are necessary if there has been any sexual contact with others: It is imperative for sexual addicts to change their email address and cell phone numbers immediately. I get more resistance from sexual addicts about this action than any other. I hear what a nuisance it is or how impossible it will be for them to make these changes. These changes are inconvenient. But sexual addiction is a disorder that causes many unpleasant things to occur. It should not be a surprise that some of the tasks of recovery are as displeasing.

Getting a new cell phone number and email address are necessary if there is just one person from the period of addiction who knows how to contact you. Also resign immediately for any social networks. If there were any contacts through company email, you should consult the company human resources department and ask if it is possible to get a new email address. Eliminating a business email account is frequently not a good option because the email remains listed in directories, multiple websites, yellow pages and more and would disrupt business communications. However companies are adept to block specific incoming email and allow accepted email to pass. Be prepared to offer HR an explanation as to why the names should be blocked.

If the cell phone is provided by the company, you may need to consult with human resources for help in getting a new phone number assigned. These changes may create some difficulty with your company but they are necessary to help you break free from your addiction.

Addicts may say that this will not be necessary because "everyone knows I'm in recovery and they are not to call me anymore," or that this is not necessary since weeks or months have passed since there was any contact with an acting-out partner. But leaving the possibility open for a former partner to contact you is inviting a slip or relapse. If a former partner calls and you are not in a strong place the chances of giving in to sexual behavior are great. Even if you are in a strong place as far as your recovery, you will need to tell your partner about this contact and that will surely add tension and stress to a relationship that is already strained.

End all secret accounts. The first day of recovery should also be spent closing all "extra" emails accounts, getting rid of secret cell phones and pagers and closing any secret post office boxes, as well as any secret bank and credit card accounts. The web of deceit and deception must be completely eliminated. The best time to make the most significant gains in changing behavior is at the beginning of recovery.

Delete all screen names and profiles. Screen names that were used for acting out should be eliminated from all computers you have used for acting out. This will involve cleaning all of the "cookies" off the computer or wiping the computer clean of all identifiers. Any "handle" that was used in a chat room and any profiles that were used in chat rooms or dating services should be erased. The recovering addict must not return to any the haunts of his addictive behavior, be they real or virtual.

Dump the pornography "stash." Any "stash" of pornography must be disposed of immediately. If you have videos or DVDs hidden in your home or office, a thorough search must be made to make sure all of them are found and eliminated. This should be done under supervision of a trusted friend, accountability partner, sponsor, or someone from a 12-step group. This procedure may also necessitate having the hard drive of your computers professionally "cleaned" to remove all traces of past acting-out behavior.

Make a commitment to recovery. The first day in recovery is also a day to make a commitment to stay in recovery and do whatever it takes to be free from acting out. This commitment will have to be solidified on a daily basis throughout recovery. It is important that from the very beginning sexual addicts make a commitment to themselves that they will be ruthless in their pursuit of recovery.

See a psychiatrist. Early in the recovery process I believe it is useful for the recovering addict to be evaluated by a mental health professional to see if there are other disorders present that need to be treated in order for them successfully address the sexual addiction. Mood disorders such as depression and other mood disorders, as well as anxiety disorders, and Attention Deficit Hyperactivity Disorder (ADHD), and others are frequently present with sexual addiction. If so present, a visit to psychiatrist is indicated. These are often managed through medication. If any of these disorders are present and are not effectively managed as part of an overall recovery strategy, it may be difficult, it not virtually impossible, for sexual addicts to have success stopping their acting out.

Read about sexual addiction. From the start of recovery, sexual addicts should develop a habit of reading all that they can about sexual addiction and recovery. Reading this book is a good start. You must become knowledgeable about the addiction that has so devastated your life. At the end of this book, you will find an extensive bibliography along with websites and addresses of agencies and organizations dedicated to overcoming sexual addiction.

Daily spiritual disciplines. Without help from God, or acceptance of a Higher Power, or simply a belief in life having an overall meaning, I believe it is impossible for a person to end all acting out and live in continued sobriety. I know many disagree with this and believe that an individual can "pick himself up by his own bootstraps." In all my personal and professional experience, the role of faith in a greater force than oneself is undeniable for continued sobriety.

The members of 12-step fellowships recognize the importance of calling on God or "a Higher Power," to do for them what they cannot do for themselves. Each individual is free to believe in the god of his or her choice. In terms of recovery from addiction, what matters is not whether we are Christian, Jew, Moslem, Hindu, or members any other religion or sect, but that we recognize there is something greater than all of us that can be accessed to lead us through the shadow of addiction to the light of sobriety.

Daily physical disciplines. Two important disciplines in successful recovery include getting regular sleep and daily exercise. Sleep should be for a minimum of seven hours per night and preferably eight hours. Often sexual addicts do not get enough sleep because they spend so many of the late evening hours acting out on the Internet or watching movies on the cable or satellite after the rest of the family are in bed. If there is a history of insomnia, it may be advisable to see one's physician to address the sleep problems. In some cases a "sleep study" may be indicated to help restore a normal pattern and level of sleep.

There are other physical disciplines that should also be cultivated, such as maintaining a healthy diet, regular dental checkups, and annual physical exams. Often when persons are active in their addiction they neglect these important disciplines, either because their acting out is taking so much of their time or that they neglect to think about their physical health and personal appearance.

Things to avoid. Healthy living dictates the elimination of tobacco in any form. Caffeine is a stimulant which is prudent to be curtailed or eliminated from one's diet. Alcohol should also be limited or eliminated. Illegal drug use should be ended, and prescription medication that is taken on a routine basis should be scrutinized. Is the medication still needed? Can it be eliminated without negative health repercussions? Your physician should make the decision for you regarding prescription medications.

Boundaries around one's work. Recovery may mean an immediate change in one's daily work routine. Some people are working with former acting-out partners. The ultimate solution to this very uncomfortable situation may be to change jobs. Others have crossed some boundaries with some employees that need to be reestablished at the beginning of recovery.

Another boundary surrounding one's career has to do with the number of hours worked. Is it necessary to work as many hours as usual? Some people may observe some workaholic behaviors that need to be addressed. A point comes when a person crosses the line from being a conscientious employee to being obsessed with work performance.

Become a careful consumer of media. Sexual addicts find that they need to be careful about what they allow to come into their minds through the media. Certainly there are suggestive movies and TV shows you will not want to watch. This is not because someone else is scrutinizing your viewing habits, rather, you acknowledging that much of what passes for entertainment is a threat to your sexual sobriety.

For some recovering sexual addicts, this means no longer listening to a particular type of music. For others, this means that there are certain songs that they choose not to listen to. This decision is especially relevant if certain music was used when acting out or even in the rituals leading up to acting out.

Some cities have a "free press" newspaper that often contains interesting articles. However, some of them also print the so-called "adult services" ads used by sexual addicts for locating their preferred acting-out behavior. In such cases, it is important that addicts protect themselves by simply having a personal boundary of not reading anything in those publications.

Have fun. In the midst of recovery life may take on a somber tone. Recovery is certainly serious business that requires many hours of work each week. That doesn't mean people can't relax. If anything, the recovering addict will find that life free of addiction is rich with discovery.

Chapter 4

Addressing the Partner

Cynthia's Story

Cynthia married Hershel four years ago. Their marriage was not perfect but it had been satisfying for both. As far as she knew, Hershel had been faithful to her. But when she went to the doctor for her gynecological exam she discovered she contracted a sexually transmitted disease. She had not been with anyone but Hershel and got a clean bill of health on previous exams.

She confronted Hershel when he got home from work. He vigorously denied any sexual involvement with anyone else and became incensed with the accusations. But over the next several weeks, Cynthia found evidence on his computer that Hershel was corresponding with multiple people for sexual liaisons. When he realized he could no longer deny his behavior, Hershel admitted having a long-term sexual addiction that involved high-risk sexual behavior with men and women, and most were strangers.

Why does the sexual addict do it?

When you discovered your partner's compulsive sexual behavior, you probably asked many "why" questions. Why does he do those things? Why can't she be satisfied with me? Why doesn't my partner love me enough to stop that behavior?

On top of these questions are other questions: What did I do to cause this? How did I fail my spouse? Did this happen because I am not attractive enough? Did I cause this by not being more sexual with my partner? How can I get him or her to stop acting out?

Is there any hope for our relationship? How can I be sure he doesn't go back to that behavior in the future?

This chapter covers these and other questions. It begins addressing why the sexual addict continues the compulsive behavior. This is an especially troubling question if you have caught your spouse or partner acting out in the past and he promised to stop. The short answer is sexual addicts continue their compulsive behavior because they are addicted to it.

A lot of misinformation about sexual addiction persists. Since the publication of the first edition of *Out of the Shadows* by Dr. Patrick Carnes in 1983, hundreds of thousands of men and women have recognized their own sexual addiction and those of their spouses and partners.

One misunderstanding about sexual addiction is that when people say they are a sexual addict, they are freed from responsibility for their actions. Nothing could be farther from the truth. The diagnosis of sexual addiction helps explain why a person will risk losing so much to pursue sexual activity. But sexual addicts remain totally responsible for their actions. The addict's best action is to have boundaries around certain behaviors in which they will not participate.

Other misinformation about sexual addiction is that all sexual addicts are "perverts" or sex offenders. While sex offenders may also be sexual addicts and some sexual addicts may commit criminal sexual offenses, most sexual addicts are not sex offenders. The typical sexual addict today may or may not be involved in viewing Internet pornography and compulsive masturbation. They may or may not be involved in sexual behavior with other people. And their behavior may or may not include any number of hundreds of specific sexual behaviors. Most of these people are not a threat to society and are not involved in any predatory activities.

Rebecca's Story

Rebecca discovered her husband's acting out. She found on his computer that he left open his email account with numerous pornographic emails he received from various women. Rebecca discovered that most of the emails were responses to sexual emails that had been sent by her husband. She was devastated by her discovery.

The question she continued to ask herself is why her husband had gone somewhere else for his sexual fulfillment. She was sure it had something to do with her. Wondering what she did to deserve the hurt her husband had caused, she sought the services of a therapist. The therapist suggested that it might be helpful if she got some new lingerie and became a bit more adventurous in the bedroom. This furthered Rebecca's belief that her husband's acting out was her fault. *The therapist's suggestion was not only completely wrong, it was harmful to Rebecca!* In truth, Rebecca was not at fault for her husband's acting out. She did not cause it and nothing she did could change his behavior. Her husband made the choice to act out and it was not the result of anything Rebecca did or did not do.

Unfortunately the misguided suggestion by Rebecca's therapist is not an isolated incident. Counseling professionals who do not have expertise for treating sexual addiction often make inappropriate suggestions that changing the partner's behavior will cause the compulsive sexual behaviors to stop.

Perhaps you have asked yourself why your spouse is not satisfied with you or how you have failed to satisfy his or her desire. What have you done that has caused your partner to seek other sexual outlets?

Your spouse's behavior is not your fault. You did not cause it. Nothing you said or did resulted in your partner becoming a sexual addict. That may be hard to accept, especially if your partner reminded you of a fight that the two of you had or of a cruel remark you made. Sexual addicts will often point to such situations, which they manufacture to provide them with an excuse to act out as the "reason" that they sought sex outside of your relationship.

There may be many factors that contribute to a person's decision to act out sexually. And there may even be traumatic things that happened, particularly in childhood, which helped shape the decisions they made. But sexual addicts have to take responsibility for their own decisions and their own actions, and for the accompanying consequences. Accepting responsibility for their actions is a prerequisite of recovery work.

You did not cause the addiction even if you look at your life and believe there are extenuating circumstances that may have contributed to your spouse's or companion's behavior. Your partner is responsible for his or her behavior and cannot avoid responsibility by using excuses: "He just doesn't understand me," or "She doesn't want to have sex as often as I do." Your partner made a choice. He chose to get involved in sexual behavior that has now become compulsive and is very destructive to your relationship. There are many things that may contribute to a person's choice to act out, but the bottom line is that person and no other made that choice to act out. You are not responsible for it, but you can take charge of how you are going to respond it.

So if you have been told that you caused the sexual addict's behavior, take solace in the fact that she made this decision alone. This may be difficult when you review your past words or actions that may have been less than loving and nurturing. The fact remains that in spite of circumstances, the sexual addict alone made the decision to pursue the addiction.

How can you get your partner to stop acting-out sexually?

Just as you did not cause the addiction, you cannot cure it. There is nothing you can do to stop the behavior. However, you can take care of yourself and determine that you are going to get healthy. You can also insist that the only way you will continue in the relationship is if your partner stops acting out immediately and engages in a program of recovery. You will need help in establishing and maintaining boundaries. Having good boundaries is essential to the two of you being able to have a lasting relationship together.

Some individuals enter recovery because they know it is the only opportunity they have to save the relationship. For their recovery to be successful, they will have to shift their focus. When a person gets to the point where he or she is willing to do whatever it takes to get free from compulsive sexual behavior, whether the relationship survives or not, then the addict is at a place where recovery has the greatest chance of success. Establishing new boundaries of what is acceptable to you and what is not may help your partner make the first important move toward recovery.

Finally, you may be wondering if your relationship has any hope of surviving. Things may look very bleak, especially as you learn the sordid details of your spouse's acting out. The good news is that there is indeed hope for your marriage or intimate relationship not only of surviving but even thriving if your partner commits to recovery, and if both of you determine that you are willing to do whatever is necessary for your relationship to survive.

Unfortunately, some people are not willing to do the work necessary for the relationship to survive. They look at the pain they have already endured and decide it is just easier to end the relationship. When faced with trauma, they want the pain to stop and the easiest way to do that is by ending the relationship. Yet even if they do end the relationship, there is still work that both partners will need to do if they are going to be able to be successful in a future relationship. Recovery is worth the effort! When a sexual addict is ruthless about achieving recovery and the significant other in her life is willing to help work on the issues together, they can achieve a new trust and reciprocal respect unknown to many other couples whose relationship was never fundamentally tested.

If my partner is a sexual addict, why isn't he or she more sexual with me?

One reason sexual addicts don't have sex as often with their spouses is because their acting out drains energy from the marriage. They are sexual with other people or they masturbate compulsively and that literally drains their energy and lessens any sexual desire they have toward their partners.

Some sexual addicts are never sexual with other people but confine their acting out to viewing pornography, engaging in sexual cyber chat, or phone sex. And with all of these forms of behaviors, they usually masturbate.

A male sexual addict may say, "My wife thinks I have been unfaithful, but all I do is look at pornography and masturbate." From his perspective, he believes he has been faithful. But from the wife's perspective, she sees his activity as unfaithfulness because he is choosing to be sexual with pictures of people (or by having sexual chat or phone sex) rather than to be sexual with her.

It is true that men and women may view sexual behavior around pornography, sexual chat rooms, or phone sex differently. Some men want to adopt a definition of unfaithfulness that includes only intercourse with someone other than their spouse. And thanks in part to memorable comments by a politician about oral sex, these men want to convince others that only intercourse qualifies as fitting the definition of "having sex." But their female partners often view any sex outside of their exclusive relationship as being unfaithful. The male sexual addict mistakenly thinks, "She doesn't understand that looking at pornography and masturbation are harmless."

Perhaps you have thought there must something wrong with you if your husband or wife is having sex outside of your marriage and having little or no sex with you. Maybe you think your partner's sexual addiction is your fault. Perhaps you have even been told that the reason your partner is sexual outside of your relationship is because you are not sexy enough, you complain too much, or in some other way the focus and blame from their behavior is shifted to you.

This is classic "blame-game" behavior for a sexual addict. Addicts convince themselves that they are not responsible for their behavior but are victims of a bad marriage, an unloving spouse, a stressful job, or any of hundreds of excuses. He or she may really think that all that is needed is the "right" partner and the acting out will cease.

Other single sexual addicts think the solution to their acting out is to get married. They believe their problem is due to their not having a steady and safe sexual outlet. So they decide the best solution is to get married, thus insuring them a sexual partner and, they hope, permanent relief from their desire to act out.

However, for an addict, the problem is not that sex is not as plentiful as he or she hoped, but rather the sexual high comes from the neurochemical release that is found in compulsive sexual behavior. Even if the addict finds a partner whose sexual appetites are similar to his own, continued sex with the same person over a period of time results in more normalized neurochemical levels. What some call the "adrenaline rush" or more accurately an increased level of dopamine, cortizol, norepinephrine, and other neurotransmitters diminishes. The lower level of neurochemical reinforcement does not satisfy the addiction. While they are now married and have a willing partner for sexual fulfillment, they are not satisfied. They look for other partners or for other means of securing higher neurochemical levels in the brain, such as engaging in high-risk sex or sexual practices that are degrading, dehumanizing, or even illegal.

It is common for sexual addicts who are married to partners with very high sex drives to opt for a low level of sexual activity, so that weeks or even months will pass without any desire for sex. In a number of cases, I have known young, healthy individuals to forgo sex with their partner for years, choosing instead to satisfy their sexual needs with compulsive sexual behavior outside of what the partner thought was a committed relationship. At least, they do not have a desire to have sex with their relationship partners. Instead, they look for other sex partners and often get as much of a rush out of the pursuit as they do out of the sexual activity that appears to be their goal.

Why do they continue to pursue other avenues of sexual expression when it appears that they have all that they could ask for waiting at home?

Because the goal of their sexual activities is not intercourse or sexual release; they are actually craving a neurochemical fix. Some married sexual addicts believe the way for them to stop acting out is to find a partner who will "love me as I deserve, give me sex any time I want it, and not nag me about doing things around the house." In short, they have the emotional maturity of adolescents who want to have all of the fun that life has to offer without assuming any of the responsibilities. Whether they are married or not, and regardless of whether their partner has a high sex drive or a more normal or even low sex drive, they will continue to seek to get high by engaging in one or several of a wide variety of sexual activities. Again the goal is not sex but rather to get their "fix."

There are other sexual addicts who believe that the "cure" for their sexual addiction will happen as they get older. They have the mistaken belief that they will outgrow their compulsive sexual behavior. But I assure you that based on a number of sexually addicted people I know who are in their 70s and beyond, sexual addiction is not something that a person will necessarily outgrow. Age may bring some moderation in certain activities and perhaps even a lower frequency of sexual activity, but it does not cure sexual addiction.

Compulsive Masturbation

Maurice's Story

Maurice had never been sexual with anyone other than his wife. Raised in a very conservative family, Maurice did not date much as a teenager. With his family's very strict religious beliefs he did not feel he was allowed ask questions about sex or even to gain any real sex education. His parents did have "the talk" with him when he was fifteen. His father told him that when he was married that he would get very close to his wife and that their resulting relationship would produce babies.

More confused than informed, he found out some sex education from friends. And to further fill the information void, Maurice started looking up sexual topics on the Internet. He found that he could get information on any sexual behavior and could even find photos and videos of people engaging in various sexual acts. That early search for knowledge turned in to a time-consuming addiction by the time he was married. When his wife finally caught him looking at pornography online, he had developed a habit of engaging in cybersex behaviors for at least two hours a day. Most of his behavior was limited to browsing pornographic websites but he recently has been following conversations in sexual chat rooms.

While he has not yet engaged in chat with anyone, Maurice was considering engaging in what he considered to be harmless chat. While online he was masturbating, sometimes multiple times a day. A few times he masturbated to the point of injury. Lately, Maurice's wife has complained that he is just not interested in sex with her and she wonders why not. He realizes that he needs to stop this behavior because of the negative impact it is having on his marriage. But so far he has not been successful in being able to stop his compulsive masturbation or his use of online pornography.

The whole question of masturbation is one that is difficult for some people to talk about. Studies show that virtually all men and a significant portion of women have masturbated at one time or another. There is an assumption that masturbation is something individuals outgrow as they leave their teenage years. In fact, a number of people, both men and women, continue masturbating throughout their adult lives.

Masturbation not only may have a negative impact on the sexual relationship in committed relationships but it may also impact communication and conflict resolution skills. Why do I say this?

How can masturbation damage a relationship outside of the sexual realm?

The answer is that women and men approach sex differently. Women typically require an emotional connection with their partner if they are going to have sex. If problems or conflict exist in the relationship, they must be addressed before many women are willing to be sexual.

It is a different story with men. Men don't have to have an emotional connection to have sex. They can completely separate sex from love or emotion. If a man wants to be sexual but there is some emotional baggage in the relationship, his wife will probably want to "unpack" that baggage before being sexual. If a man is not willing to wait or make the emotional investment in the relationship, he can masturbate — literally be sexual with himself and not have to expend any emotional energy.

The dismal fact is that too often men will continue to indulge in masturbation and neglect the emotional and communication concerns of the relationship. For too many men, masturbation becomes a compulsive act that is used to medicate pain, stress, loneliness, fear, anger or other emotions. For that reason, masturbation within a committed relationship can become a selfish act and may contribute significantly to the couple having a lower than desired frequency of sexually intimate moments.

Perhaps the biggest problem with masturbation is that it is often the ignition for other acting-out behaviors. Before frequenting sexual massage parlors, before the clandestine affair, before seeking out prostitutes, many addicts rationalize their behavior by saying that they were engaging only in masturbation and fantasy. In other words, they see the self-gratifying action as pertaining only to themselves and not to their spouse or partner as a statement of rejection or withholding of pleasure. The neurochemical reinforcement provided when one masturbates to a fantasy is powerful. The resulting brain chemistry gives a person a high not unlike the high that comes from using certain illegal drugs.

Promises, Lies, and More Promises

You caught him looking at pornography several times. Each time your partner has made promises to stop it and never do it again. Or you found out your partner had an affair (or perhaps another affair). Again, promises were made that the affair would end, but you have evidence that it is still going on. What do you do? Will you ever be able to trust your partner again? That is the question that nags at the core of your being. You want to trust the person you love, but you have found that there is a web of deception between the two of you and you wonder if your partner will ever be truthful with you.

It has often been stated that a person cannot be a good sexual addict without being a world-class liar. This is not a character assassination but a statement of fact. An addict lies not only to cover up acting out, but to preserve the image of herself that the unsuspecting spouse or partner has. Sexual addicts believe that if their partners knew everything they had done in the past as well as their current acting-out behaviors, they would not stay in the relationship.

And if this is true of your own discovery of your partner's acting out, you, too, have had thoughts, or are thinking about leaving the relationship. But I encourage you to stay with it and give recovery a chance.

The frustrating thing is that sexual addicts will often lie not only about their compulsive sexual behavior but about some small and virtually meaningless things. When asked questions concerning why they were late, what happened to a broken flowerpot, or other relatively unimportant questions, sexual addicts will often lie. Truth-telling is an important part of the recovery process.

Why does he or she lie (even about little things)?
Lying may be the toughest habit for your spouse or partner to break. For some sexual addicts, even after they have stopped acting out and have started doing significant work in recovery, they find lying to be a habit that is difficult to sever. The frustrating part of lying is that the sexual addict may lie even about the most inconsequential things. For example, you ask your partner if he remembered to put out the trash, he might lie and tell you that he did, even though he did not. In his mind he may rationalize that he can get it taken care of before you get home so it really does not count as a lie.

Why do people lie?
Initially, lying may be a survival skill. If a child has a parent who is abusive and perhaps even caught up in his or her own addiction, a

child may lie to keep from being abused. Or if a child is neglected, ignored, or in some other way marginalized, he or she may lie to get attention. Sometimes children with a learning disability or another limiting factor may lie to appear more normal.

Lying learned in childhood is often difficult to stop. It may be carried into adulthood and be among the hardest of habits to break. People may lie as self-defense. They shade the truth to make themselves appear in a better light. Some people invent a web of deception to make themselves appear more interesting or more successful in hopes it will make people like them more.

Many partners wonder how far the lying extends. "If she lied when she said she was on a business trip, how do I know she is not lying when she says she loves me?" After the first revelation of acting out, partners find that their familiar world begins to come apart. The person they thought would never lie to them has not only been caught lying but has been caught in sexual behavior that has shattered their trust.

Discussed in a later chapter, polygraph exams can be useful tools for helping a sexual addict cultivate the habit of telling the truth. Sticking to a regular schedule of follow-up exams after a formal disclosure as an integral part of therapy, and reinforces the habit of living within the truth. As the sexual addict continues in recovery, he or she will come to recognize the invaluable necessity of truth-telling skills, even if those skills are imposed by the partner as conditions for not leaving the marriage or relationship.

Is it my fault?

They may have told you repeatedly that their acting out is entirely your fault. Your partner may have said unkind things to you including that you are not attractive to her, that she does not love you (perhaps never has), that you have "driven" your partner to the compulsive sexual behavior, and other similar things. When a sexual addict is in the midst of her addiction, it is common for her to say some of the most cruel and heartless things imaginable.

Sometime addiction first comes to light after the birth of a child. When some mothers are giving themselves to the task of taking care of the new addition to their family, they suddenly discover that their husband is misbehaving sexually. His addiction is especially difficult for a spouse to take if she has put on weight in recent years or if she is now showing some of the affects of aging that were not present when she met her husband. More than ever, she needs appreciation, affection and loyalty.

If you are a woman to whom this has happened, you might have said to yourself, "Maybe it is my fault my partner is acting out with other people." Regardless of what may have happened in your life or what your partner may have said to you, his addiction is not your fault. You did not cause it.

In the past (fortunately, this does not happen often today), some well-meaning therapists have advised women to get some sexy lingerie or to have sex with their partner more frequently as a way of controlling his behavior. Even in churches there is the same misinformation being propagated as a solution to a man's unfaithfulness. I have heard ministers say that it is the woman's job to be sexual with her husband every time he wants sex. This suggestion not only does not solve the problem of sexual addiction, it actually feeds the addiction. Healthy sexuality dictates that people are only sexual when they feel like being sexual. A woman should not feel under any obligation to be sexual at times or in situations where she does not feel valued and loved. This is true for men as well. Although much of what constitutes sexual addiction in the social environment is predicated by men, women are increasingly becoming addicted within the home environment, where the access to the Internet allows them to be concealed behind the anonymity provided by a pseudonym and they can act out their own fantasies that before would have been impossible.

As your partner's addiction has come to light, you may have tried in various ways to make yourself more attractive for her. And you may doubt yourself because your efforts to stimulate his interest in being sexual with you have been rebuffed. Perhaps your spouse or partner has even laughed as you or otherwise been cruel to you.

An important truth: You cannot control the sexual addict's behavior. There is nothing you can do that will result in the sexual addiction coming to an end. Your partner will not stop acting out even if you increase the frequency of your sexual encounters several fold. A whole wardrobe of provocative clothing will not cause him to end his addictive behavior and be sexual only with you.

If the addiction is being fueled by pornography and masturbation, a natural consequence is for him to have less desire to be sexual with you. Your attempts to impact the addiction by being sexier only result in you feeling cheap and foolish. They will not deflect his destructive behavior. The addiction concerns the addict directly. It is his fault. It is his choice. You did not cause the addiction. But you can be part of the solution by taking care of yourself, setting good boundaries as to what is acceptable and what is unacceptable in your relationship; and by doing your own recovery work, all the while encouraging your spouse or partner to embrace recovery.

Why do sexual addicts do the things they do?

You caught her again! And once again your partner promised that the addictive acting out would stop. Your spouse seems no less sincere than the first time she was caught. It just does not seem to add up.

Why would sexual addicts return to acting-out behavior when they know that such behavior is damaging, possibly destroying their marriage or intimate relationship?

The only adequate explanation as to why people continue such behavior in the face of such negative consequences is that they are addicted. For many people, both addicts and partners, the term sexual addict finally explains why a person would return to such "incomprehensible and demoralizing behavior," as the AA "Big Book" says. Sane people would never risk their health, their relationship, their job, or, literally, their freedom for something as transient as sexual arousal. Yet we must assume that the five to six percent of all Americans who are sexual addicts are not thinking clearly due to their addictions. Isn't that insanity? One can see how a doctor having too many drinks at a party risks his life, that of other drivers on the road, and his entire network of family, friends and patients by thinking he can make it home "on automatic pilot." It is that same form of "insane" thinking that leads the sexual addict to believe his or her actions are under control and are no one else's business.

In fact, addiction is about indulging in some of the most insane behavior in an effort to acquire the next "fix." Nothing and no one matters to an addict as much as the next high.

Sexual addiction is often marked by insane behavior but sexual addicts themselves remain solely responsible for their actions. No one "made" them pursue their sexual activity. It is unacceptable for addicts to turn their acting out toward their partners and say, "When you got angry and yelled at me, you made me look for love and comfort some other place."

True, there may be many circumstances in relationships that a sexual addict does not like, but that individual alone is responsible for his or actions. No one else forced the partner to act out sexually. The sexual addict chose to act out and alone bares the total responsibility for the outcome of those actions, no matter how one is provoked.

In fact, recovery is impossible until sexual addicts face their behavior, stop blaming anyone else, and determine that they are going to be accountable for their actions.

Is sexual addiction compulsive or impulsive?

The answer is both. Sexual addiction may include compulsive and impulsive behaviors. Certainly there is a compulsive element to sexual addiction. Behaviors are repeated over and over again as sexual addicts look for the "high" they received from their past acting out. Rituals often accompany the acting out so that addicts may wear the same clothes (or "lucky" underwear), cruise the same parts of town, spend hours surfing the Internet, or engage in other behaviors that are so regimented that it is almost as though the sexual addict is following a script written by someone else. As one women said, "I was unable to stop using the Internet until the sun came up," or one male sexual addict said, "When I finished with one prostitute I would immediately begin seeking the next."

There is also an impulsive element involved in sexual addiction. For most sexual addicts, there are times when they find their acting out triggered by something, then follow through with sexual behavior they had not planned. The unexpected phone call from a former sex partner or opening an email only to find pornography are the sorts of difficulties with which sexual addicts must contend. And without a good personal recovery plan, proficiency in using the tools of recovery, and experience in keeping healthy boundaries, many such individuals find it difficult to resist the impulse to act out. Will power alone is not enough to overcome a pattern of addictive behavior.

The individuals in question never set out to act out. In fact, they may have made promises to their partner and even a vow to God that they will never again act out. But then an impulse triggers them and they succumb to the same destructive behavior they swore they would never repeat. Triggers may include seeing a provocative advertising poster, passing a sexually-oriented business, getting a phone call or email from a former acting-out partner. For the sexual addict, as for all addicts, the addiction itself is always within reach--unless one averts one's gaze, stops the idle fantasy and pushes it away, be it a bottle of alcohol, a box of candy, an illegal drug, or a pornographic website.

If my spouse is a sexual addict, is there any hope for our relationship?

The answer is a qualified "Yes." The bad news is that sexual addiction is one of the toughest addictions to conquer. (I use that word advisedly for it is never truly conquered but it can be kept at bay for life.) Crack cocaine addiction is often thought to be the most difficult addiction to address, but the crack addicts I have treated who are also sexual addicts tell me that their crack addiction was not nearly as difficult to get relief from as was sexual addiction.

The good news is that sexual addiction responds well to treatment. While I believe treatment from a competent sexual addiction specialist is of paramount importance in recovery, some sexual addicts never receive any kind of therapy or treatment and are able to achieve and maintain sobriety through 12-step fellowships. These groups, patterned after Alcoholics Anonymous (AA) go by names such as Sex Addicts Anonymous (SAA), Sexaholics Anonymous (SA), and Sex and Love Addicts Anonymous (SLA). (See appendix for a list of 12-step fellowships dealing with compulsive sexual behavior.) The biggest determining factor in a person's success in recovery is his or her willingness to "go to any lengths," as the Big book of AA says, to get free from compulsive sexual behavior.

For your relationship to survive after entering recovery, both you and your partner must be willing to do whatever it takes to make the relationship work. That will entail a lot of hard work for both of you, and it will require a willingness to stick with the relationship even when your friends or family members encourage you to leave. As long as your spouse or partner is actively pursuing recovery and you are doing your own work in therapy and organizations like Co-SA or S-Anon, there is reason to believe that your relationship cannot only survive addiction, but will actually thrive in recovery.

While there is no guarantee that your relationship will work, my experiences as a psychotherapist have shown that when both partners were committed to the relationship and actively pursuing recovery, most of those relationships do indeed survive addiction. It is common for clients who are entering their second or third year of recovery to state that their marriage is not only better than it was prior to the revelation of the addiction, but that it is actually better than they ever dreamed it could be.

Is addiction a choice?

This is a difficult question to answer. Some choice is involved in a sexual addict's behavior. Each person is responsible for the choices he makes. But addiction is a powerful drive.

I have known men and women who were aware of the risks involved in their acting-out behavior but continued anyway. There are those who have been fired from multiple jobs for accessing pornography at work. I have known men who have repeatedly contracted sexually-transmitted diseases and put their health and that of their partners' at risk by habitually engaging in dangerous sexual behavior. It is common to learn that sexual addicts have destroyed multiple marriages due to acting out.

Why would a person return to risky behaviors in the face of such loss and pain?

The only thing that adequately explains such behavior is addiction.

Sexual addiction is more powerful than many people imagine. Only the addict knows the terrible force of the addiction. It is like undertow that is always waiting for the moment when the individual wades into what appears to be the most innocuous act.

Although sexual addiction may be the most difficult of all addictions to break, recovery is not only possible, it is well within the reach of all sexual addicts if they will give themselves completely to the task of recovery.

Could my partner be gay or lesbian?

Sonny's Story

Sonny had been happily married for fifteen years. His wife had twice caught him in affairs and had been devastated by the knowledge that he had been emotionally involved with other women. Sonny did not want to hurt his wife anymore but did not feel he could completely stop acting out. He reasoned that the greatest problem was not that he was having sex outside their marriage but that he was involved with other women. Sonny thought that he could get some of the same sexual fulfillment with men, so when he traveled on business, he sought sex with men by posting ads on various websites that had a personals section. Sonny believed himself to be heterosexual and even noted that when he would have sex with a man, the only way he could climax was to watch heterosexual pornography as the same time.

Sonny is not gay. His acting out with men is something that he did for convenience and with a belief that it was not as great of a betrayal to his wife. He just wanted to have sex and he found a host of willing male partners who did not want a relationship but were also just seeking a sexual release.

What do you do if you find out that your husband is acting out with men or, in the case of your wife, other women?

It is a complicated issue. In terms of men acting out with other men, some women feel a bit of relief knowing their husband's acting out is not with women, while other women experience an extra measure of pain. For women who feel relieved, they may reason that their husband's behavior is not as much of a personal affront to them since their husband didn't look for sex with another woman. But for a number of women, the homosexual behavior brings additional questions, confusion, and perhaps shame.

Upon finding out he has been having sex with men, the first question some women ask is if her husband it gay. Surprisingly, the answer is not necessarily "yes." There are numerous reasons that men might have sex with other men. Certainly one of the reasons is that he would describe himself as gay. If he is gay and chooses to live as a gay man, then each member of the family would benefit from some significant support (perhaps including psychotherapy for each person) as he walks a new path and the rest of the family copes with his decision.

But not every man who has sex with other men is homosexual. I realize that sounds somewhat confusing and perhaps you are even thinking this cannot be right. There are heterosexual men who choose to have sex with other men.

The purpose of this chapter is not to determine if a man is heterosexual, homosexual, or bisexual. There are numerous books devoted to this. Rather, this section has you consider the possibility that same sex acting out is not the touchstone criteria to determine sexual orientation.

But if your husband is heterosexual, how do you explain the fact that he has been sexual with other men?

There are several reasons heterosexual men may have sex with other men. One of those reasons is to reenact past trauma that he experienced. If your husband was abused by a man or by a boy older than himself, he experienced some trauma as the result. One of the dysfunctional ways of dealing with that trauma is to repeat the traumatizing event or events with other men. Many of these men are not conscious that they are reenacting their past trauma. They do not have feelings of attraction for other men or yearn to have an emotional connection with them. All they know is that they have a desire to be sexual with men. As with all victims of abuse and trauma, it is important for these men to seek psychotherapy to cope with that past trauma.

Another reason men may have sex with other men is because they are seeking a greater thrill because they consider this activity forbidden. The more forbidden, the greater the risk, and the greater the neurochemical reinforcement from the sexual activity. Rather than behavior they consider perverted repelling them, they become attracted to that which they once loathed.

Some men have sex with men because they are seeking some sexual behavior they either do not experience with their partner or believe they would be criticized for seeking from their partner. Again, part of the thrill is crossing into the forbidden zone of sexual behaviors. They are able to get their sexual wants met without having to risk being rejected or ridiculed by their partner.

Still another reason heterosexual men may have sex with other men is because they may find a greater availability of partners or at least they perceive that to be so. Public restrooms and parks have long been the hunting ground for men who are looking for male sex partners. The Internet brings multitudes of people willing to have anonymous sexual encounters into a public space. When some heterosexual men realize this, they become aware that sexual encounters are often available with little or no planning and may occupy only a few minutes of their time.

Heterosexual men may have anonymous sex with men because they feel the lack of emotional attachment makes those relationships safer. They have sex with other men because they rationalize that it is not cheating in the same sense it would be if they were having sex with a woman. They may tell themselves that they are still being faithful to their wives because they are not involved in a relationship that involves love or emotional attachment. Surprisingly, there are some women who also feel less threatened if their husband is having sex with men instead of women. They may feel that since their husband did not seek out another woman their marriage is not at as much at risk.

Up to this point, I have discussed the issue of the spouse or partner being gay or lesbian. When homosexual acting out occurs in a heterosexual relationship, in the majority of cases it concerns the male partner. Due to many causes, from the nature of male sexuality to social contexts that recognize gay behavior, men can cross over more easily into gay life and return to their perceived heterosexual identity more easily than women can when crossing into a lesbian environment. Traditionally, if a woman goes outside the relationship it is not to seek sexual pleasure per se, but emotional communication. In terms of what men and women need in a relationship, a sense of dialogue, trust and understanding are usually more necessary to women than to men, who are typically quicker to separate their feelings from their passions. By my experience, emotional intimacy precedes physical intimacy for women, whereas for men it needn't be present. However, more women are creating alternate lives on the Internet, either with men or with women. Nevertheless, it is more common for a heterosexual married man to indulge in occasional gay affairs than it is for a woman to have a lesbian relationship while married to a man.

The difference is one of emotional commitment and duration. A man doesn't need to make the same commitment of time and attention developing a relationship that a woman requires.

These conditions may change in our society as more and more people create alternate identities on websites. It is difficult enough for most people to maintain a sense of integrity in a world where deception, deceit, and illusion attempt to distract people with sophisticated advertising, offering everything from a better vacation spot to the latest computer or MP3 player. For the addict, though, the noise of temptation can be practically deafening.

Dealing with Trauma

Lucy's Story

Lucy found out about her partner's clandestine sexual behavior six years ago. She confronted him and he told her it was all in her head. He convinced her that she was going crazy and that there was nothing going on. Any time that she would mention to him that there were things about his behavior that did not make sense, her partner would yell at her and tell her she was stupid and insecure.

Two months ago, she confronted him with additional evidence that this time he did not even try to deny. He said he was relieved that he had been caught and that he was going to do all that he could to get free from all of that destructive behavior forever. And as far as Lucy knows her partner is doing a good job with his recovery.

However, Lucy's problems were just beginning. Sleep comes slowly for her now and when it does it is often fitful. She awakens often with nightmares involving her partner's sexual behavior.

Some days she cannot eat. On other days Lucy is ravenous and devours any food in sight. She finds that staying busy helps so she fills her days with activities and tries to think positive thoughts. But in unguarded moments Lucy breaks down into tears for no apparent reason. At other times she is gripped by fear but cannot pinpoint an event that has made her fearful.

Lucy finally saw a therapist who was well acquainted with sexual addiction and with the impact of sexual addiction on partners. The therapist explained to Lucy that she was suffering from deep psychological trauma and suggested that she might have post traumatic stress disorder, or PTSD. Lucy protested and said this could not be the case since she had never served in the military and had not survived some type of catastrophe. Yet her therapist told her that there was now a significant amount of evidence that some people who are in relationships with a person who acts out sexually can develop PTSD. For those partners who do not have PTSD, the effects of significant psychological trauma still need to be addressed for them to heal.

In the past, much of the focus for the partners of sexual addicts has been on recognizing and stopping codependent behaviors. However, I believe your greatest need after discovering your partner's sexual addiction is to give attention to the way you have been wounded by the addictive behavior. More attention is given to the subject of trauma in chapter ten.

Chapter 5

Addressing the Couple

In this chapter, I use "You" to mean both the addict and the spouse or companion, for in a relationship you are as one. It is that unified force of love, spirit and trust that must be brought back to health through recovery.

Recovery means simultaneous hope for both of you. It means hope that your marriage or intimate relationship will not end and can be restored. Recovery means hope that you can be trusted and can fully trust your partner again. This journey also brings hope for the fairy tale ending — "and they lived happily ever after."

After being in recovery for several months, it is common to hear spouses say of their partners, "We are happier than we have ever been." This is especially gratifying because the journey they have been on and how much healing has had to take place for that statement to be true. Regardless of how bad things are in your relationship at present, regardless of how much trust you have lost, there is hope for you.

Even if you cannot fully embrace this hope now, trust when I say that after helping sexual addicts free themselves and their loved ones, I have convincing proof that life can be different. If you engage in recovery without reservation, it is possible to regain the relationship you lost and thought it not possible to save.

Is there any freedom to be had on the recovery road? I wouldn't have devoted most of my life to helping sexual addicts and their loved ones regain love and respect, their very lives, unless I believed totally in freedom from addiction. I would not have written this book unless I wanted to reach sexual addicts everywhere.

No matter where you are reading this, no matter how dark is the place where sexual addiction has taken you, I want you to know that freedom is ahead if you commit yourself fully to the dual dimension of recovery. The wife, husband, companion of a sexual addict, are essential to the recovery process.

The addict has a much harder road to take alone. Your presence adds comfort and strength during the process. However, the recovery is not freedom from addiction. It is more accurate to say what is waiting is freedom *within* the addiction.

Countless times I have observed a great truth: When the sexual addict embraces recovery, when it becomes an all consuming passion, he will achieve freedom from compulsive sexual behaviors. Within a relatively short time the individual suffering the addiction will find that life can be free of acting out. This may come as the fulfillment of a dream. Prior to recovery, many sexual addicts believe they will never get free from the demoralizing and often dangerous behaviors of their addiction. Some are reconciled to the belief that they are not capable of being monogamous. Others are resigned to the belief that their addiction would eventually put an end to everything that was of value to them.

Again, the freedom a man or woman experiences in recovery is not freedom from addiction. That is, most addiction experts believe that addiction is something that will continue to follow a person throughout life. That does not mean that they will struggle daily with whether or not they will act out. Rather, it means that they must forever remain vigilant to the divisive and surreptitious nature of addiction and not return to their destructive behaviors.

They must realize that they can never take their behavior for granted. There will be places they will never again be able to visit. They will always need to avoid some movies and television shows and they will likely even have to forgo listening to certain songs or perhaps whole categories of music because it was once closely tied to their acting out.

These boundaries are not imposed by you, the spouse or partner or a therapist, or a 12-step sponsor. Instead, when sexual addicts have gotten fully into recovery and begin to understand what is required for the recovery journey, they impose boundaries on themselves in order to be able to live with what has been described by sexual addicts themselves as a caged tiger.

The freedom that you both will ultimately experience is freedom from fear. You, the addict will no longer have to lie or be deceitful. And, you, the partner, will no longer have to question the truthfulness of those areas that have caused so much pain in the past.

If you become fully engaged in recovery and are willing to do whatever it takes to get "sexually sober" and stay that way, you will find that the fear of acting out will diminish. As you commit to the recovery process, you will eventually realize that you are living free from deceptive behavior.

The recovery journey requires that an addict learn to live in the truth. This may ultimately prove to be more difficult than the ability to stop acting out. Lying and deception become intertwined with daily life. But recovery will ultimately bring freedom from deception as the sexual addict learns to speak the truth in all areas of life.

Chapter 6

Recovery Components

Recovery Timetable

How long will recovery last? Some experts say it is a three to five year process. Your recovery may be longer or shorter. There are multiple factors that affect how long recovery lasts and determine the type and duration of treatment.

The crisis that brought about the initial search for recovery must be great enough to motivate the sexual addict to be willing to look for help beyond self. It is not enough that life has become difficult or that there is discord in the relationship. It typically takes a significant crisis to propel a sexual addict to take the recovery plunge.

Another noteworthy factor in determining the length of the recovery process is the spouse's willingness to aid in recovery. Understandably, there are partners who refuse to do any work in recovery. They reason that since the addiction pertains to their spouse or partner, it is up to him or her to get "cured." Sadly, such partners fail to see that their own pain and trauma is being prolonged by not also being willing to enter recovery.

From a relationship standpoint both partners need to be willing to do their individual recovery first, and then be willing to work on the relationship if it is to have and hope of restoration. The relationship may be the first thing a couple wants to see restored. However, individual recovery is foundational to couples recovery. Recovery progresses through readily identifiable phases. With each phase the sexual addict and partner move toward the goal of completely arresting the addiction and restoring the relationship.

As recovery progresses, the sexual addict and the partner will be able to determine if solid recovery is taking place by checking their progress against the *Hallmarks of Good Recovery* (see p. 76). In the process both will produce a *Personal Recovery Plan* (see p. 78) as a guide to their progress.

Recovery Phases

Survival Phase	This phase begins when recovery begins and lasts from 6 months to 1 year or more.
Stability Phase	Begins from 6 months to 2 years into recovery and lasts 1 year or more.
Sustaining Phase	Begins from 1½ to 3 years into recovery and lasts 1 year or more.
Freedom Phase	Persons in this phase have been in recovery for 2½ years or more. This is the ultimate phase one aspires to in recovery.

Survival Phase

This is the beginning of the recovery journey. The Survival Phase lasts from six months to a year or more. This phase does not begin until a person recognizes himself as a sexual addict and is willing to get help. The early months of recovery are often significantly impacted by the presence of the dual enemies of recovery — denial and resistance.

Denial is a defense mechanism that sexual addicts use in order to be able to live with themselves in spite of the presence of behaviors they abhor. To keep from being plunged into the depths of despair, sexual addicts become skilled at denying not only that they are addicted to sex but that there is anything wrong with their behavior. They may cite numerous examples in society and especially in entertainment that validate their belief that they are normal and just "doing what other people are doing."

This denial is so strong that some sexual addicts can live in this state for years without giving much thought to wanting to stop their compulsive behavior. Tragically, some are never able to break free from denial. They live with the belief that their behaviors are typical of others and they ignore all evidence to the contrary.

Resistance is a defense mechanism firmly entrenched in sexual addicts who resist all effort of their spouse, their family, and friends to get them into recovery. In therapy, resistance results in slow or no progress at all. It is typical for a client who is resistant to treatment to challenge therapeutic interventions and assignments. Clients who are highly resistant believe they know best what treatment they need and think they have great insight into their addiction. They may even go from therapist to therapist as they shop for someone who will agree with their own treatment philosophy.

There are a number of reasons that addicts have resistance. The most common is that they may view the term sexual addict as being so negative that they will avoid identifying themselves with that term at all costs. For others, they resist treatment because they do not believe anyone else is like them and therefore, they do not fit into treatment plans that are designed for other sexual addicts. Some individuals are resistant because they think they will have to give up sex for life and they do not believe that will be possible.

Resistance and denial present challenges in treatment. Only when sexual addicts are able to break through both of these defense mechanisms are they able to make progress in recovery. Some sexual addicts continue to exhibit resistance and denial for several years, resulting in little change in their behavior and great frustration for their partner.

The focus of therapy in this phase of recovery is on stopping all acting-out behaviors. The common denominator in this phase is usually a crisis. A crisis often leads a person to enter recovery. If the crisis is viewed as temporary or just an inconvenience, sexual addicts may wander in and out of this phase over a period of years before actually beginning the recovery process. Group therapy is typically started a few months into recovery as an adjunct to individual therapy.

It is at this point sexual addicts first attend 12-step meetings related to sexual addiction and see a therapist about their addiction. Some individuals believe life as they know it ends at this point. And perhaps it does. If all they have known is sexual addiction and out-of-control compulsive sexual behavior, then that acting-out life is coming to an end. The crises in their relationships, or their jobs, or in the legal system, have finally gotten their attention and they are desperate for help.

While this is usually the beginning of the journey, persons who have suffered a slip or relapse are also in the survival phase. While a slip or a relapse does not mean a person loses what they have learned in recovery thus far, it does mean that there must be a return to those basic principles of recovery that set the stage for further recovery work.

Also in the survival phase are persons who have been in recovery for some time, but are currently experiencing a crisis related to their former addictive behavior. Therapy in this phase focuses on stopping all compulsive sexual behaviors and also lays the foundation for future recovery work. This is a time for establishing solid sobriety and being able to identify a sobriety date on a calendar. During this phase, all immediate crises are addressed and a preliminary plan for recovery is mapped out.

The focus of therapy for couples work in this phase is in understanding the role each partner plays in recovery. It may be a while before any real trust is regained, but at least there can be work in this area that can ultimately result in a full restoration of trust in the relationship.

As the recovering sexual addict moves out of this phase he or she will have firmly established evidences of sobriety. All compulsive sexual behaviors will have ended. The individual will be engaged in regular recovery routines, including attending two or more 12-step meetings each week and meeting weekly with a sponsor.

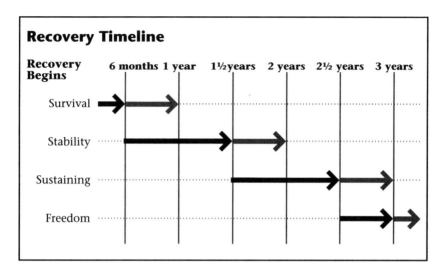

Recovery Timeline

Recovery Begins	6 months	1 year	1½ years	2 years	2½ years	3 years
Survival						
Stability						
Sustaining						
Freedom						

Stability Phase

This phase of recovery begins six months to two years into recovery and lasts for a year or more. Persons in this recovery phase have a good understanding of recovery and are regularly engaged in the recovery basics. They attend meetings regularly and have a sponsor. They are actively working with their sponsor as they progress through the steps as outlined by the 12-step fellowship with which they are affiliated.

The focus of therapy in this phase is on making recovery routines life-long habits. Clients typically have broken through all of their denial and resistance and are making solid progress. They look forward to attending 12-step meetings and recognize therapy as something that is enhancing their recovery rather than a punishment for previous bad behavior.

Another important focus of therapy in this phase is on relapse prevention. It has been said that getting sober is not difficult but staying sober is. With this in mind, therapists help equip clients with tools for dealing with triggers and threats to sobriety. Clients are prepared for various recovery challenges and for taking greater responsibility for their own recovery.

It is during this phase that traditional couples therapy can begin. (The therapy with couples during the earlier survival phase focuses only on crisis management.) Communication techniques are taught and couples learn basic dialogue techniques that allow them to communicate with each other without blaming and shaming. Conflict resolution is also taught during this phase.

Several significant things have happened in recovery as a client moves to the next phase. First, he will have made a complete disclosure of all of his acting-out behavior to his relationship partner. He has taken and passed a polygraph exam to verify that the disclosure is accurate and complete. Next, the client will be living "slip free" and has been free from all acting-out behaviors for at least six months. At this point sexual addicts do not see the tools of recovery as a burden, but as means of achieving freedom and restoring integrity. Partners moving out of this phase are actively working on their own recovery and the relationship has been stabilized around recovery norms.

Before moving toward a polygraph exam, it is crucial to read the next two chapters. Polygraph can be a helpful tool in recovery when it is part of an integrated therapeutic approach. Used by itself, polygraph is not necessarily helpful to recovery and may indeed be harmful. A complete discussion of the appropriate use of polygraph exams is found in chapter 8.

Sustaining Phase

This phase of recovery begins 18 months to three years into recovery and lasts for one year or more. Disclosure has been accomplished and the relationship has been stabilized. Sexual sobriety is solid and growing.

The focus on therapy during this phase of recovery is on deepening the addict's knowledge and broadening the foundation of recovery. Therapy may move from a weekly to a biweekly routine. Clients at this phase have assumed total responsibility for their own recovery.

Couples therapy during this phase is focused on understanding and developing healthy sexuality. This is an often overlooked subject in recovery but one that demands attention. It is not enough that all compulsive sexual behaviors be stopped. Couples must learn how to relate sexually in a healthy manner.

As a client moves out of this stage of recovery, he has worked all of the steps of recovery in one of the 12-step fellowships. The recovering sexual addict will be free from all acting-out behaviors for a minimum of one year. By this time, his anger and resentment are well-managed and the relationship with the spouse or partner is growing both in the rebuilding of trust and intimacy.

Freedom Phase

Persons in this phase of recovery have been in recovery for two and a half years or more. They typically spend the first six to 12 months in this phase actively working on recovery. Clients in this phase ultimately move out of therapy or use therapy sporadically to address specific concerns, work on "rough spots" in their relationships, or do periodic recovery checkups.

The focus of therapy during this phase is to fine-tune recovery routines. Tools and recovery techniques that were learned early in recovery are reviewed. There is an emphasis on establishing balance in the client's life.

Work with couples in this stage is focused on deepening and expanding skills learned earlier. Communication and conflict resolution techniques are reviewed. There is a major emphasis on boundaries as well as continued work in the area of healthy sexuality. As clients move out of therapy, they will have been free from all acting-out behaviors for at least two years. By this time they are actively sponsoring others and are otherwise engaged in giving back to the recovery community. They have developed and implemented a strong maintenance plan for continued recovery.

The time comes for therapy to end when the relationship is stable and growing. The relationship is not without conflict, but the couple has learned to resolve conflicts without attacking or shaming each other. Trust has been substantially and perhaps completely restored in the relationship.

With measured steps, hope has led to freedom.

Recovery is something a person does! The word "recovery" can be used in many ways as it pertains to sexual addiction. Recovery can describe the goal of a person and also one's state of mind. The word can be used to describe the journey one takes in getting his life back. Ultimately, recovery is both a state of mind and a set of actions. While individuals say they are "in recovery," unless there are recovery actions to back up that statement, they are at risk of losing their sobriety and returning to their compulsive sexual behavior. What does good recovery look like? Persons who are in recovery are busy doing the work of recovery. When a person is in recovery, there are many evidences of recovery activities.

Hallmarks of Good Recovery

At the beginning of recovery, I provide the individual with an understanding of sexual addiction and also give him an overview of recovery. In the first or second therapy session, I lay out the various action items that are involved. There are things to be done immediately, as well as things the recovering sexual addict will need to do daily, weekly, monthly, and annually.

Start attending 12-step meetings. From the first day of recovery it is essential to take significant steps to address the addiction. The first thing the addict must do is to find a list of 12-step groups that support sexual addiction in her area.

You can find a list of these groups in the appendix. It is important to attend a minimum of two 12-step meetings a week. Many recovering addicts find attending 90 meetings in 90 days (a "90/90"), an effective way to establish sobriety.

Get a sponsor. A sponsor is a person who will lead the addict through the 12-steps of recovery. Sponsors are recovering addicts who have themselves worked all 12 steps of recovery with a sponsor of their own and have a significant period—ideally a year or more—of sobriety. Often this person volunteers an hour of time each week over a period of many months to meet with the addict. Sometimes these relationships last for several years. Regular meetings with a sponsor should be part of one's ongoing recovery routine.

A sponsor's role is to provide accountability for the sexual addict and also to mentor him through the 12-steps of recovery. When a person first reads the 12-steps, it is not apparent that working these steps involves a significant amount of work. While there is not one right way to work the steps, each sponsor has his own approach to methodically guide addicts through a series of exercises over a period of several months to a year or more. After completing this work with a sponsor and maintaining sobriety, the addict is then qualified to become a sponsor and guide other recovering persons through the steps of recovery.

Circle of Five. The addict is encouraged to establish a Circle of Five—a group of five people of the same gender to whom they will always be accountable. The members of this circle know all about her addiction and will be open to frequent contact with her. One of the individuals can be a recovering addict's sponsor. Another might be her accountability partner from a church or synagogue. The recovering addict then enlists three other persons to whom she will be accountable on a regular basis. Typically, these might be other persons in recovery whom the individual can immediately contact if necessary.

A Circle of Five is particularly important for men since they have a tendency to isolate themselves and to try to handle problems on their own, whereas women are more relational and are more comfortable sharing their feelings with other women. This reluctance to be open is why some men refuse to ask directions or ask a neighbor for help moving a heavy object. Men are often acculturated to believe they need to handle things by themselves and that it may even be a sign of weakness to ask for help.

When a man is struggling with compulsive sexual behavior, he often becomes more isolated. He frequently will stop having contact with friends. He may even cut himself off from family members when his acting out is at its peak.

With a Circle of Five, if a sponsor moves out of town, a client's recovery has not been so negatively impacted that he is in danger of a slip. Certainly, the individual needs to get another sponsor just as soon as possible, but he can still get continuing accountability from the other members of the circle until a new sponsor is enlisted.

Begin therapy with a addiction therapist. Is it mandatory that a sexual addict engage the services of a psychotherapist for recovery? The short answer is "no." In fact a significant portion of addicts do not use the services of a therapist. And for persons who simply cannot afford therapy, they can do solid recovery by utilizing 12-step groups and maintaining a regular working relationship with their sponsor.

But it is also true that many sexual addicts struggle to establish and maintain sobriety. Often therapists are able to help recovering persons establish a better recovery foundation than they could get without therapy. If you choose to use a therapist, be sure you select a therapist who is skilled in working with persons who struggle with compulsive sexual behavior. Good places to begin this search are on the website of the Society for the Advancement of Sexual Health (www.sash.net) and the International Institute for Trauma and Addiction Professionals (www.iitap.com). Therapy with a sexual addiction therapist should begin immediately and should continue for two to three years. A combination of individual and group therapy create an effective way of treating sexual addiction.

Personal Recovery Plan

While there are many elements to recovery and no two recovery plans are exactly the same, it is important for each person in recovery to come up with his or her own *Personal Recovery Plan* (see p. 84) in consultation with his/her therapist. Each plan will include a list of actions to be taken on a daily, weekly, monthly, and annual basis. The plan is developed under the direction of a therapist.

After clients have put together a first draft of their *Personal Recovery Plan*, they are guided through the following checklist to see if there are additional things that need to be added. Recovery is most successful when multiple routines are built into regular daily and weekly activities. The more routine they are, the more effective recovery becomes.

It is crucial that both the sexual addict and the partner develop their own personal recovery plans. Many of the items covered below in *Recovery at a Glance* are specific only to the sexual addict but some, such as seeking therapy, attending 12-step groups, as well as the physical and spiritual items are also applicable for the partner.

Recovery at a Glance

A Weekly Recovery Record that allows you to measure your individual progress toward Hope and Freedom and information on audio CDs covering specific periods of the recovery process are found at the end of this book These "virtual fireside chats" are meant to strengthen the resolve of you and your partner during times when you are tested or in need of inspiration.

Immediately

- Change cell phone number. The only exception is if this number has never been used in acting out and/or contacting acting-out partners.
- Change email address. The only exception is if this address has never been used in acting out and/or contacting acting-out partners.
- Get "blocking" and "tracking" software. (See links to helpful software at www.hopeandfreedom.com.)
- Close all "extra" or secret email accounts.
- Close all secret bank and credit card accounts.

- Eliminate pornography "stash." This step should be taken with the help of a sponsor or someone else in recovery. The additional accountability afforded by this person will lessen the possibility of descending back into the addiction. Your goal is to lay a good foundation of recovery.
- Make a commitment to stay in recovery and do whatever it takes to be free from acting out!
- See a psychiatrist: many sex addicts suffer from depression or other disorders that can make recovery difficult or impossible if not treated.
- Purchase and read *Out of the Shadows*. (See the Recovery Related Books link at www.hopeandfreedom.com)
- Attend an "S" group meeting today. (For 12-step fellowships and meeting locations in your area see the Appendix.)
- Get a sponsor (you will find sponsors at a 12-step meeting).
- Get an accountability partner (from your church or community group).

Daily Plan

- Read the daily meditation from *Answers in the Heart,* (See Recovery Related Books link at www.hopeandfreedom.com) (Whatever your spiritual beliefs, be sure and embrace the spiritual aspect of your life during recovery.)
- Morning prayer for sexual sobriety and recovery. Just a simple request like, "Thank you for a day of sobriety yesterday. Help me to live soberly today."
- Do "Step Work." Your sponsor will lead you in working the steps. This process may take up to a year.
- Read "The Big Book" of "S" group, cover-to-cover and over again. This text is published by each of the 12-step groups that focus on compulsive sexual behavior. In each book, you will find information about the distinctive features of that group as well as practical recovery suggestions.

- Read other recovery material; begin with Patrick Carnes' books, 12-step literature, etc. It is a good practice to keep a recovery-related book on your night stand and spend a few minutes reading about recovery every night.
- Restrict or eliminate TV watching. A good exercise at the beginning of recovery is to make a log of your weekly use of time. Keep track of how much time you spend in each activity by quarter hour increments. It is often surprising how much time is wasted in watching television and in non-productive surfing of the Internet.
- Strictly limit computer use. Beyond what is required for your job, determine the maximum amount of time you will spend on computer entertainment pursuits daily. Set yourself this boundary and rigorously maintain it.
- Avoid music and movies that do not support recovery. For some this may mean they have to eliminate a particular genre of music. For others there may be selected songs as well as movies that they choose to avoid in the interest of their recovery.
- Develop healthy eating habits.
- Avoid caffeine.
- Limit or eliminate alcohol.
- No illegal drugs. Prescription drugs only as directed.
- Get regular sleep and a minimum of 7-8 hours a night.
- Make daily recovery-related journal entries.
- Affirmations: claim a new affirmation every morning and repeat that affirmation out loud at least one hundred time during the day. Positive self-talk must take the place of negative thoughts and destructive self-talk.
- Evening meditation or devotional. If married or in a committed relationship, do this with your partner.
- Evening prayer for sexual sobriety and recovery.
- Joint therapy session with partner (seeing the therapist working with you in your sexual addiction).

Weekly Plan

- Individual therapy session.
- Group therapy (usually after being in individual therapy for a few months).
- Attend a minimum of two 12-step meetings. Many sexual addicts find attending 90 meetings in 90 days ("90-90") a good way to establish sobriety.
- "Service work" for 12-step meetings.
- Meet face-to-face with your sponsor.
- Meet face-to-face with an accountability partner. (Usually someone in your church, synagogue, or community group.)
- Get a Circle of Five
- F.A.S.T.T. Check-In with partner (Explained in detail in chapter 12.)
- Make a minimum of two "program calls" (phoning other persons in recovery to talk about recovery progress—good practice for an emergency).
- Physical exercise minimum three times a week for 30 minutes.
- Worship or some other weekly spiritual discipline: don't neglect the spiritual dimension.
- Do something "fun."
- Date night with spouse or significant other.

Monthly Plan

- Review all journal entries for the past month.
- If not in regular weekly therapy, consider having a monthly session as a point of accountability.
- Joint therapy session with partner (if in a committed relationship)

Annual Plan

- Marriage enrichment seminar/conference (if married).
- Weekend retreat for men only or women only: attend at least one retreat (12-step, therapist led, or spiritual retreat a year).
- Physical exam. Physical health is often neglected while living in addiction.

You may find this list daunting. Remember, your sexual addiction is deeply ingrained and has become a way of life. It will take considerable effort to overcome your destructive habit patterns. If this seems like too much work, perhaps you are not ready for recovery. Hopefully, you and those you love will not have to suffer much more before you get ready to make recovery a way of life.

Personal Recovery Plan

What I need to do with regard to recovery, physical health, spiritual and mental well-being, and for my relationship

Things I Commit to Doing for My Recovery

Daily	Weekly
1. Morning prayer for recovery	1. Attend ＿＿ 12-step meetings
2.	2. Meet with my sponsor
3.	3.
4.	4.
5.	5.
6.	6.
7.	7.
8.	8.
9.	9.
10.	10.
11.	11.
12.	12.
13.	13.
14.	14.
15. Evening prayer for recovery	15.

Monthly	Annual Activities/ Commitments
1.	1. Physical exam
2.	2. Dental checkup (2x)
3.	3.
4.	4.
5.	5.
6.	6.
7.	7.
8.	8.
9.	9.
10.	10.
11.	11.
12.	12.
13.	13.
14.	14.
15.	15.

Chapter 7

Disclosure

Daniel's Story

Disclosure often brings terror into the heart of both the sexual addict and the partner. Daniel dreaded disclosure from the first time he heard someone mention it in a 12-step group. While he did not mention it then to his partner Teri, he was fearful that she also might hear about disclosure, and if she did, he was sure that she would insist that he do a full disclosure to her of all of his acting-out behavior. There were many things that he had never told another soul. And he was sure if Teri knew what he had done since they had been together that she would leave him. Not only were there things he had never told her but he purposely hid the magnitude of his acting out in the years before he met Teri.

He recalled when they were telling each other about their sexual history. He listened to Teri as she told him about her previous sexual encounters. Daniel sanitized his sexual history so that it would match Teri's and, in his mind, make him more acceptable to the woman with whom he wanted to share the rest of his life. When he finished, Teri remarked that she was surprised he had not been involved in more sexual behavior. He replied that he had been saving himself for her. But now he was fearful she would eventually find out the whole truth about his sexual behavior and he was sure that would mark the end of the relationship.

There are relationships that end after disclosures. However, they did not end because of the disclosure process itself but because of the revelation of the acting-out behavior that had been previously concealed. It is also true that when a disclosure is done with the aid of a skilled sexual addiction therapist many relationships not only survive but can ultimately thrive after acting out has been stopped, significant recovery has been accomplished, and trust has been restored.

The Indispensable Ingredient

Disclosure in recovery is a clinical process of revealing all of one's past acting-out behaviors to end secrets and restore integrity. A disclosure is made with the desire of putting an end to acting out and having an opportunity to bring restoration to the relationship.

Disclosures that are incomplete are not disclosures. As stated earlier, they are more accurately called "deceptions."

What is disclosure?

The American Heritage Dictionary defines disclosure as

1. The act or process of revealing or uncovering.
2. Something uncovered, a revelation.[12]

There are different types of disclosure. As a sexual addict begins working with a sponsor in a 12-step group, the individual needs to be open and honest with his or her sponsor about all behaviors. Some 12-step groups ask members to do a public First Step where they chronicle all of their sexual behaviors before the rest of the group. This is one example of disclosure.

Other disclosures may be made to one's children, parents, or other family members as well as to selected close friends or employer. There is a Twelfth Step disclosure a sexual addict may do to someone else struggling with compulsive sexual behavior to encourage him or her to seek help.

Disclosure that is the focus of this chapter is the truth-telling that a sexual addict does to his or her partner during recovery. In this disclosure, the individual tells his or her partner every part of his or her sexual history, omitting nothing. As a clinical procedure, disclosures are carefully planned and require a significant amount of preparation. With assistance of a skilled sex addiction therapist they are done in a therapy session.

To many people, even the mention of the word disclosure brings a mix of fear and promise to both sexual addicts and their partners. There is debate in 12-step groups about the advisability of doing a disclosure. Some people in recovery advocate for it and others that believe it is harmful to recovery. In some 12-step meetings there may be persons strongly opposed to doing a disclosure. They recount "people they know" who have done a disclosure that turned out badly. They may tell of their own experiences with disclosure and the damage they believe it did to a relationship.

Some speak with passion about how the Ninth Step says amends are to be made only when they will not harm others. Others refer to this as the "Ninth Step slide," pointing to speculation that Bill W., a founder of A.A., added the words to the Ninth Step that amends should be done "except when to do so would harm themselves or others," to keep from telling his wife about his extra marital affairs. Some individuals believe that disclosure will harm their spouse and themselves if they reveal all of their acting-out behaviors.

Recovery is a program of rigorous honesty. How can one be honest and not tell the whole truth to his relationship partner about his behavior during their relationship? The "Big Book" of Alcoholics Anonymous (1976) states that those who don't recover are people who are "constitutionally incapable of being honest."[13]

However, disclosure is not "step work," but rather a treatment procedure used in therapy as an important element of recovery.

Disclosure used in sexual addiction recovery is not the addict unloading all of his shame and guilt onto his spouse or partner, or other members of a sexual addiction meeting. It is not a lengthy conversation in the bedroom where a spouse or partner describes a series of sexual transgressions.

Rather, disclosure should be a clinical procedure that is carefully guided by a therapist in a clinical setting. It is conducted according to specific guidelines which will be covered in detail later in this chapter.

There are some missteps in disclosure, alluded to earlier: the "let it all out" method where the sexual addict unburdens of all the lurid details of past sexual exploits without the aid and direction of a sex addiction therapist. This flow of confession is damaging if the partner is not prepared to hear and does not have any psychological protection after the disclosure. To worsen the experience, this type of disclosure is usually incomplete, inflicting further trauma on the spouse when the addict recalls added details of acting out.

Another misstep is a disclosure before the addict is ready to be completely truthful. Deception is so ingrained in sexual addicts that it often takes a period of time before the addict is ready to be completely open with the therapist. It is amazing how many incidents of acting out I hear a year after starting therapy from addicts who said that they previously told "everything." It sometimes takes even longer for sexual addicts to get to the point where they are ready to be truthful with spouses and themselves!

Disclosures should be conducted only after the addict has stopped acting out. If there is any doubt, disclosure should be postponed. If the addict is not ready to make a break with past behavior, the disclosure will have to be repeated, further traumatizing the partner.

An additional mistake is for a disclosure to be made without an addict carefully examining his past. It is helpful for a recovering addict to do a careful reconstruction of past sexual history prior to disclosure. When reviewing sexual history with clients, it is common for them to say that they had completely forgotten certain events until we start working together to uncover their past behaviors. Often the reason they have such difficulty with their memory is they spent years trying to forget what they have done. Denying past events and forgetting them is one way they cope with bad behaviors.

One of the most devastating errors in disclosure is in making partial or progressive disclosures. Some addicts prefer making a partial disclosure, in an attempt to minimize damage to the relationship. If later on they deem their partner strong enough, they may reveal additional information. In fact, partial disclosure is worse than no disclosure at all.

One research study found that multiple disclosures are common and damaging. In 1998, Drs. Jennifer Schneider, Debra Corley and Richard Irons surveyed sexual addicts and their partners. They discovered that the majority of sexual addicts (58.7 percent) and their partners (69.7 percent) reported more than one major disclosure. In some of the cases, the intention was for the first disclosure to be sufficient, but revelations of additional acting-out behavior prompted another disclosure.[14]

Disclosing to the wrong person is another mistake in disclosures. After reaching the point of recognizing their addictive behavior and how destructive it is, some addicts decide to "come clean" with their employers. They reveal that they have not been as productive due to their addiction. In some cases, recovering addicts feel compelled to tell their employer they used company time or perhaps a company computer for acting out.

As genuine as the motives may be to reveal this sexual behavior to one's employer, they often have negative consequences. One reason is that sexual addiction is not well understood by most employers and not covered by benefit plans or employee assistance programs, as is alcohol or drug abuse. Unfortunately, the response of many employers to learning an employee is acting out sexually is immediate termination.

A disclosure to an employer may be premature or inappropriate. Clients should wait before approaching their employer about their compulsive sexual behavior. If a disclosure is indicated, there is adequate time to do this in the future. I encourage clients to wait until their Eighth and Ninth steps in their 12-step work and let their sponsor help them explore the options for making amends to their employer. In some cases the amends may come in the form of a donation to a charity in the name of the employer. Or in cases involving theft, full financial restitution may be made anonymously. Often sponsors encourage the restitution to be larger than the amount that was stolen or wasted.

Another well-intentioned but misguided disclosure is to disclose to casual friends. Recovering addicts may be so excited about their new-found freedom that they are tempted to blurt out virtually to everyone about being a sexual addict in recovery. While one can praise their enthusiasm and wish to share their progress, the potential of such disclosures to turn out badly outweighs the temporary joy received from telling others about their recovery journey.

Another mistake is disclosing to the children any details inappropriate for a child's age. It is also not advisable to make a disclosure to children before making a disclosure to one's spouse.

When making a disclosure to children, the parents should do this together. It is important for children to have an opportunity to hear from the addict about the behavior and recovery rather than having the partner disclose it. Disclosures must be age-appropriate, and in all cases disclosures to the children, even if they are adults, do not require the same details as disclosures to the spouse. The disclosure should focus on the fact that the improper behavior of the past has stopped and the parent is in recovery. Equally important is for the spouse of the addict to refrain from shaming or blaming language in front of the children.

Disclosures often follow a predictable course. First, there is complete denial by the addict. Even faced with irrefutable evidence, some addicts adamantly deny any wrongdoing. Some faced with photos of their car in front of a strip club deny that it is their vehicle. When it is pointed out that the car has their license number, they insist the photo was altered. There are women, who having received expensive gifts from acting out partners, concoct stories to attempt to explain the gifts and shield the sexual behavior.

Anger often follows denial. The anger may take the form of self-righteous indignation when confronted addict says; "I can't believe you would accuse me of such things!" Anger may be followed by a wall of silence.

Sensing he may no longer be able to get by with alibis, the sexual addict may make a partial disclosure after being caught, followed by new alibis and additional partial disclosure of acting-out behavior. The final step in the journey is when a full and complete disclosure is made. This is possible when life becomes unbearable or, more accurately, as he goes through life while locked in the throes of addiction. When a sexual addict gets to the point of committing to a full and complete disclosure, he can make significant gains in recovery.

The Hope and Freedom Disclosure Process

Disclosure Procedure

The following is the procedure used by Hope & Freedom Counseling Services during disclosure. Other sexual addiction therapist's disclosure procedures may be different.

Hope & Freedom Counseling Services use disclosure in two ways. The major focus is working with a couple in a Three-Day Intensive. The therapist guides the sexual addict through disclosure preparation in the weeks prior to arrival at our center. Usually the same therapist works with both the sexual addict and partner throughout the intensive following the procedure described below.

An alternative is to work with one person in one or two individual therapy sessions per week over an extended period in preparation for the disclosure. Concurrently, another therapist prepares the partner to receive the disclosure. After preparation is completed, we coordinate the schedules of the couple and therapists typically blocking out a half a day for the process. A polygraph examiner is scheduled to arrive and conduct a polygraph exam immediately following the disclosure.

On the day of the disclosure, each partner meets with his or her therapist for final preparations. For the partner, this is a time to make sure she is in an open frame of mind and is ready to hear whatever is disclosed. She is reminded to listen during the disclosure without interrupting or asking questions.

The therapist will often ask the partner to prepare a list of questions to ask following the disclosure. These may be questions about unexplained absences, missing money, suspicious behavior, secretive actions, or questions that have been previously asked but offered unsatisfactory answers.

For the addict, the time just prior to the disclosure is used to practice reading the disclosure. Even though he has read previous versions of the disclosure aloud in every session over the past several weeks or months, this last time is more of a dress rehearsal. Often addicts find themselves far more emotional than anticipated and may have difficulty starting the reading.

This is a time to prepare the addict to listen to the questions and expressions of pain and anger that usually follow disclosures. He is taught to use a good internal listening boundary, following a model developed by Pia Mellody in *Facing Codependence*,[15] to learn to let in the truth his spouse or partner speaks and to learn how to block words meant only to hurt, which are not true. For example, addicts are taught to allow, "You have no idea how much you hurt me!" but to mentally block words, "You have never loved me!" Both may feel true, but the latter is more an expression of pain. When the disclosure session begins, the partner may select any seat in the room where he will be most comfortable. The addict is instructed to sit across the room facing the partner. Next the therapists locate their seats across from each other, such as, the couple might sit at the nine o'clock and the three o'clock positions and the therapists would sit at the twelve o'clock and the six o'clock positions. Chairs are arranged so that the couple is sitting about six to ten feet apart. If the spouse prefers, he is welcome to ask the therapist to sit closer in order to feel more support during the disclosure session.

Once the couple is in place, one therapist reads the following statement. "The disclosure process has several parts. Those parts include reading the disclosure, processing what was heard, drafting the questions that will be asked in the polygraph exam, taking the polygraph exam, and finally the polygraph report session. New information will likely be learned today. Sometimes there is additional information that comes out in each of the parts of the disclosure process. The purpose of this process is to put an end to secrets. The goal for the recovering sexual addict is to make a permanent break with his or her acting-out behaviors. The goal of the partner is to get the truth about the spouse's behaviors so that he or she does not have to imagine what sexual things may have taken place. For the couple, the goal is to lay a foundation upon which trust can be rebuilt. (To the injured partner) This disclosure is different than one that the two of you would have if you were doing it privately. It does not contain any feelings, apology, words of love, or alibis for past behavior. Certainly we hope and believe that your spouse or partner does love you, regrets his or her actions, and truly wants to be forgiven by you. However, we don't want any of these things to detract you from getting in touch with your feelings over what you hear in the disclosure. Hopefully, forgiveness will come and there will a restoration of intimacy and relationship. That time is in the future and not something that is expected or even appropriate today. Please listen to the disclosure without any interruption. After your partner finishes reading the disclosure, you may ask any questions that you like and respond verbally any way you wish. It is also all right for you to remain silent if you so choose. Following the disclosure you will have some time with your therapist to begin to process your feelings and then will have the opportunity to come back and say anything additional you may wish to say. Do either of you have any questions before the disclosure begins?"

During the reading of the disclosure, the partner's therapist takes general notes to be used later to help the partner process what has been disclosed. It is often difficult for the sexual addict to read the disclosure. A significant number of addicts have to stop during the disclosure to get control of their emotions and to recompose. Partners are instructed during preparation for this session not to be distracted by any tears even if they have never seen the addict cry before. Before beginning, the addict has been instructed to read the disclosure directly to his or her partner and to be in touch with feelings but not to do or say anything construed as a plea for sympathy.

After the disclosure is read, the partner has a chance to ask any questions that he or she wishes and to express any feelings generated by the disclosure. About half of the partners have something to say at this time. They are often stunned by what they have heard and need time to process it.

At this point, the therapists take the addict and his spouse or partner into individual therapy sessions. Each client needs to be allowed to begin to process the experience and talk about his feelings. The task of the partner's therapist is to help her think through what has been disclosed. Often there are questions about the timeline of what occurred. During this session the spouse can look through the actual disclosure if they want to. This is often helpful especially for persons more responsive to the eye than to the ear. It is also important for the partner to be able to get in touch with her feelings during this session. The therapist can help the partner focus on the impact that hearing the disclosure had on them. Additionally, the partner is encouraged to express anger, sadness, or whatever emotions are present.

After both have had time with their individual therapists, all four persons get back together in the room where the disclosure took place. The spouse or partner usually has a list of questions for clarification that were prepared in the individual session. The partner asks questions and the addict is encouraged to answer truthfully and completely. At the end of the questioning period, the partner can speak whatever feelings of anger or other emotions that are present.

After the partner is finished with the questions and whatever they have to say, the polygraph questions are written. One therapist takes the lead in this process, but all four people may have input into developing the questions. Once the polygraph questions have been finalized the addict is asked if there is anything about any of the questions that will present any difficulty for him or her. The addict is also asked if he or she needs to add anything to the disclosure. Occasionally, an individual will say, "Yes, there is something else I need to say."

It is common for new information to be revealed throughout the process and even up to the polygraph exam. Our clients are instructed that if they remember anything else while they are preparing to take the polygraph exam to tell the examiner that they have remembered some new detail. This will be included in the report session. Then the exam is completed. In that way the addict is able to express the final details and pass the exam to verify he has no more secrets. Any additional information that is disclosed to the polygraph examiner is revealed during the report session.

Sexual addicts share the belief that if their spouses knew everything they had done, they would not love them. This belief causes some individuals to hold back secrets until the very last moment. Even if this happens, the partner is prepared prior to the disclosure for the possibility that additional information may be come out at any time during the process.

The Most Important Component of Recovery

Disclosures are important for both the partner and the sexual addict. Partners have a right to know about their intimate companion's acting-out behavior. The partner's health may be at risk because of the behavior of the sexual addict. And even if the addict is not directly acting out with other people, the partner still has a right to know if he is involved in sexual behavior that could have a negative effect on the relationship.

The spouses of sexual addicts are empowered by disclosures. Upon hearing a disclosure, a spouse may say, "I knew it wasn't all in my head. I am not crazy after all. My suspicions were right on target!"

While some therapists believe the greatest value of the disclosure is to the spouse or partner, and perhaps the primary purpose for a disclosure is for the spouse to have information, there is also great benefit to the addict. Many who slip and never been able to establish long-term sobriety have never given a full disclosure. Deep examination often reveals that there are secrets they have buried and committed to take to their grave. Secrets have shame attached to them. Where there are secrets and shame, the addiction has a foothold to return. The importance of getting out all of the secrets is discussed in the chapter on polygraph exams.

Sexual addiction lives and thrives in the darkness of denial and deceit. A disclosure brings all of the secret behavior into the light. Once in the light, sexual addiction loses much of its power.

When sexual addicts make a disclosure to their spouses or intimate companions, they take a major step toward restoring their integrity. The secrets they kept reinforced the feeling that they are "bad" and continued to strengthen negative thoughts about themselves. Walking in truth is fundamental to recovery from sexual addiction.

The second of Carnes' Four Core Beliefs of a Sexual Addict in *Out of the Shadows* is other people will not care for them as they are.[16] Another way of putting it, "If it came out what I had done, my spouse would leave me." With this belief being at the core of a sexual addict's being, the idea of making a full and complete disclosure of acting-out behavior is an act that should be avoided at all costs. However, for the sake of recovery, sexual addicts must put an end to living in deception.

Timing

A disclosure is planned as early as is practical in the recovery process although it usually takes several weeks to prepare both the addict and the partner for this. There are several prerequisites to disclosure. First, the addict must have made a conscious decision to stop all acting-out behavior. If he is not sure about wanting to stop his acting out behavior, a disclosure is not helpful. A disclosure done prematurely only succeeds in needlessly traumatizing the partner. It is advisable to schedule a disclosure after the sexual addict has a good foundation in recovery and knows what will be required long-term.

There are circumstances in which it is important to put disclosure on the fast track and have it as soon as possible. If there is potential for the partner to be exposed to a sexually-transmitted disease or other health concern, it is crucial that the disclosure take place without delay. It is also important to proceed immediately with a disclosure if family members are involved in the addict's behavior. (e.g. rape, incest, etc.)

In cases where there are children involved or who may be at risk, the disclosure should be scheduled right away. When children are involved, it is vital for the addict to understand that the behaviors must be reported by the therapist to authorities. The involvement of children necessitates shifting priorities to making sure that the children have adequate protection and support before focusing on other recovery issues.

Additionally, if the addict's behavior involves someone that the spouse knows, the disclosure should be scheduled as soon as possible. The spouse or intimate companion has a right to know without any delay if his or her partner is being sexual with a friend, an acquaintance, or someone at work.

In all cases, it is important that the partner be in therapy prior to a disclosure and that the partner's therapist knows that a disclosure is forthcoming. The therapist will use this time to prepare the partner for what might be heard during the disclosure as well as to support the partner during the disclosure. Psychotherapeutic support is crucial before, during, and after disclosures. If the partner has potential for self-harm or is otherwise mentally or emotionally unstable, she must first be stabilized before proceeding with a disclosure.

It is also a good practice for disclosure to be planned after the partner has established his own support network. Twelve-Step organizations such as Co-SA, S-Anon, AL-Anon, and CoDA are an important source of support to partners during the recovery journey. The individual and group support provided by group members is invaluable not only during disclosure but throughout the recovery process.

When is it not advisable to have a disclosure?

Some sexual addicts believe they should not do a disclosure under the following conditions: if they think their partner will leave, if they believe the partner can't handle the information, if their acting out involves some behavior they consider degrading, or if their behavior involves sex with the partner's friends or family. On the contrary, disclosure should be made in each of these cases.

When is it not right to have a disclosure?

One such circumstance is if the couple is not committed to the marriage and has decided on divorce. If minds are made up that the marriage is at an end, there is little reason to continue with a disclosure to the spouse. Conducting disclosure at this point becomes fodder for divorce attorneys.

Another example is when the spouse is terminally ill. While this must be decided on a case-by-case basis, it may be advisable to focus on providing as many positive memories as possible during her remaining time. I am aware of cases where a spouse was terminally ill but still wanted to have a full disclosure. In those instances, couples felt that the potential of finally developing true intimacy in a relationship without secrets was worth the trauma involved in the disclosure.

What about those circumstances where the spouse truly does not want to know what the husband or wife has done?

While sexual addicts are quick to suggest this may be the case, few spouses prefer to remain in the dark. After partners of sexual addicts build support networks in their own 12-step group and are empowered through their own therapy, most believe that a full disclosure is important and something they want to hear.

Preparation of the Partner

Once a decision has been made that a couple is working toward a disclosure, it is important that both enter therapy with a psychotherapist skilled in working with partners of sexual addicts. The focus of this therapy is multifaceted. First, the therapist will help the partner gain an understanding of sexual addiction and realize that the sexual addict acts out because of the addiction and not from a lack of love or respect for the spouse or partner.

The therapist will also help spouses understand that the sexual addiction is not due to them. This is an important message because they may have been told repeatedly that the reason their spouse acts out is because they are not sexy enough, are overweight, do not satisfy the partner's sexual desires, or another invalid reason. The truth is the partner did not cause the addiction. Regardless of the partners' behavior or any deficiencies, their behavior is not the cause. A careful examination of a sexual addict's behavior often reveals that the behaviors predated the marriage or intimate relationship by years.

A significant objective for the spouse is in the area of empowerment that includes finances. If the wife does not work, it may be important that she consider working. Unless she is prepared to manage life on her own, and the financials involved, she will never be in a position to set boundaries concerning what behavior is or is not acceptable in the relationship.

It is important that partners have an understanding of the financial position of the family and the assets and accounts they have. They should know the details of the family's financial obligations and if they do not, they need to demand them of their spouses or partners.

As revelations of the addict are revealed it is crucial that the partner does not agree to any major changes proposed by the addict, such as moving, selling the house, or significantly increasing credit card debt. The time for making financial decisions is in the future. The immediate goal of recovery is to stabilize both partners and the relationship and not making financial decisions.

Sexual addicts confronted with evidence of their behavior may panic and start concealing financial assets. There are cases where retirement accounts were emptied, stock portfolios liquidated, savings accounts closed, and homes refinanced without the partners' knowledge. While this is not the norm, it is important for partners of addicts to be aware of this possibility and protect themselves, including legal remedies, if they suspect anything.

There may be a reluctance to consult an attorney at this stage for fear of causing a situation to escalate. However, if a sexual addict is making financial decisions without the partner's knowledge, taking legal actions is prudent and necessary. These actions do not signal an end to the relationship. Rather, it is merely the partner being vigilant and protected from irresponsible actions of the addict.

One of the most important areas of empowerment comes when a person takes time to decide what is and is not acceptable in the relationship. Partners are asked if it is appropriate for your spouse to have sex with others, which puts your health at risk. Is it right if partners have time for many "extracurricular activities" and not invest time or emotions with the family? Usually, the response is "of course not!"

Some people are put off being asked questions with obvious answers. As obvious as the answers may be, in practice, many people put up with bad behavior from sexual addicts for years because they fear that if they object the sexual addict will end the relationship. Some relationships do not survive sexual addiction. It is possible that a marriage or relationship will end when sexual acting out is exposed, and when the companion sets boundaries about what is acceptable and or not.

Boundary setting did not cause the relationship to end. Rather an addict will allow it to end rather than be cut off from sexual encounters. It is not reasonable for a person to allow his partner to be involved in sexual activity that does not include him and is not part of a healthy relationship. Fidelity is a common marriage vow. If the couple is not married, there are needs for trust and understanding essential for an intimate relationship to be maintained.

In preparing the partner of a sexual addict for disclosure, she should be reminded of the high probability that additional acting out will be revealed during the disclosure. This new information may have been long hidden or it may be relatively minor details about behavior that he or she already knows. It is common for new information to surface during the disclosure. Therefore, the partner must be prepared to receive jolt of revelation; and the therapist's job is to support the partner through the disclosure process, no matter how unsettling it is.

Partner's Response to Disclosure

Shock is the most common response to disclosure. The spouse or partner may tune out parts of the disclosure because what is revealed is too painful to accept or hear. This is why it is important for the partner to have a therapist there for support and to listen for details that might have been missed. It is the therapist's responsibility to help the spouse or partner find her voice and to process the things heard during the disclosure.

Anger is another common response to disclosure. The spouse may say things to the recovering addict, such as, "How could you?" or "You had no right to put my health at risk for the sake of your own enjoyment!" Anger needs to be expressed and channeled properly. A therapist is helpful in determining how to appropriately express anger.

Sadness is also a common response to disclosure. A person may feel that the entire relationship was a lie and that she was never truly loved. In her sorrow she may want to withdraw and not have any communication with her partner for a while.

The range of responses to disclosure is similar to the stages of grief articulated by Dr. Elisabeth Kübler-Ross in her book, *On Death and Dying*.[17] These are denial, anger, bargaining, depression, and acceptance. People confronted with their partner's acting-out grieve for the death of a relationship or at least for the death of what they believed their relationship to be.

One response that should be absent at the presentation of a formal disclosure is forgiveness. Hopefully this will come as the sexual addict makes a permanent break with his compulsive behavior. As the partner continues in therapy, he can find the right time to express forgiveness. But it is unfair to expect the spouse or partner of a sexual addict to listen to a disclosure and be immediately forgiving. The spouse must take time to process the pain and come to terms with what was revealed. This process can take months or even years.

Premature forgiveness on the part of the partner may send the wrong message to the addict. It may be misconstrued by the addict to mean he can continue acting out without working at rebuilding the damaged trust and intimacy in the relationship.

Step by Step Through the Disclosure Preparation Process

What is included in the disclosure?

Many sex addiction therapists limit the disclosure process to include all acting-out behavior starting at the time the sexual addict met his or her relationship partner. I initially followed this model but in recent years conclude that disclosures should cover all sexual behavior from age eighteen to the present.

The focus of the disclosure is on behaviors, not thoughts and fantasies. Specific time frames are included. For example, the admission may be; "In 1989 I went to a strip club for the first time." Or; "For two months in the fall of 2007 I had a virtual sexual affair on the Internet." Names of acting-out partners are not included except in cases where the spouse knows the person, or the sexual addict still has contact with that person, or in the case where the person is someone the sexual addict works with or used to work with.

Disclosures include "I" statements so that the addict takes responsibility for all of his behaviors. For example, the sexual addict should say, "I picked up a prostitute and had sex," rather than "A prostitute propositioned me and we had sex." While both sentences may be correct, the focus should be on the addict owning up to all of the behaviors and not shifting blame to someone else or attempting to lessen the acting-out behavior by highlighting someone else's actions.

The sexual addict must never shift the blame for acting out. There may be a temptation to try to project guilt onto the partner. For example, a man might say to his partner, "In August, you got mad at me so I went to a strip club and had sex with one of the dancers." Or a female sexual addict might say to her husband "Saturday, you got drunk and fell asleep on the sofa, so I went to a bar and met a guy and had sex." Regardless of the circumstances, the addict is the one who made a decision to act out.

Also, included in the disclosure are details of all anonymous sexual encounters and specifics as to the last sexual acting out and the last sexual conversation that he or she had with anyone other than the spouse or intimate partner. The addict should also give list of arrests as well as any other encounters with law enforcement officers. Dates and details of the last time he or she was involved in each of various acting-out behaviors should be included. For example, "The last time I viewed pornography was in April of last year. The last time I had sexual intercourse with someone other than you was in February of this year."

The disclosure should also include a complete list of gifts given and received from sexual partners or persons he or she hoped would become sexual partners. The recovering sexual addict should make an itemized list of all expenditures incurred in acting out plus a grand total of money spent. Included are other costs of addiction including transportation, hotels, meals, alcohol, recreational drugs, therapy costs, legal expenses, lost business, gambling losses, and any other expenses as part of the addiction.

The sexual addict should tell how he paid for those expenses and give details of any deceptions. For example: "I have a secret credit card and checking account," or "I have skimmed money out of our business," or "I always get my business expenses reimbursed in a separate check." Details of any money spent on sex partners over and above the list of gifts previously mentioned should be included.

The disclosure should also contain a list of all ways he deceived the relationship partner, for example: lying about going on business trips, deception about misuse of a company expense account, any secret stashes of money along with the source of those funds, the existence of secret post office boxes and secret email accounts, and secret cell phones with the phone number and service provider. The sexual addict should also provide a list of all screen names used on the Internet and all aliases used in the acting out.

If other addictions are involved, like alcoholism, drug addiction, or gambling, the sexual addict needs to give a detailed account of those activities and tell how they related to the acting out. Money spent on these addictions is included in the disclosure as well as a complete list of all money won and lost gambling and how the winnings were spent and losses were covered.

With all of the detail in the disclosure there are some things left out. Childhood acting-out behavior is normally omitted. The reason for this is so spouses will not lose sight of the damage their husbands or wives have done to their relationship, and begin to feel sorry for them, or give them an alibi for their behavior because they might have had an abusive childhood.

An exception to the omission of childhood sexual behaviors is in the case of incest or other events strongly associated with shame. Incestuous relationships often have significant shame attached to them. It is important that sexual addicts get these secrets out in the open. Shame and secrets provide a foothold for addictive behaviors to return. Exposing shameful secrets to the light helps break the repetitious component of compulsive sexual behaviors.

Other things that are left out of disclosures are words of apology, expressions of love, alibis, and blame of the partner or other persons. Excluding expressions of love and apology are often the most difficult part of disclosure for both the sexual addict and the partner. Both feel the need to hear these words that we often associate with owning up to a wrong. However the use of apologies or words of love during a disclosure divert the partner's attention from being injured by the sexual addict's acting out. It is important for the partner to be able fully to feel the pain of the acting-out behavior in order to begin to heal from it.

We omit blame on any co-occurring disorders like depression or Attention Deficit Hyperactivity Disorder (ADHD). There are a number of psychopathologies that may make significant contributions to sexual addiction. But it is more important that the sexual addict not do anything to avoid taking responsibility for his actions.

After the addict reads the first draft of the disclosure, he usually needs to rewrite it, leaving out the more graphic details. This is not done in an attempt to hide anything. Rather, exclusion is to keep unnecessarily explicit details from further traumatizing the partner. For example, a disclosure may have a paragraph where the addict lists the number of sexual partners during the relationship as well as a list of various sexual acts that were engaged in. The addict then would go through a chronology of when those encounters took place. This is preferable to listing each encounter and then giving a detailed account of what sexual behaviors were experienced with that person. After a disclosure is read, the partner can ask for additional details.

Sexual addiction therapists do not agree completely about dealing with explicit details. Some feel strongly that the spouse or intimate partner's right to know details supersedes the desire to protect her from unnecessary trauma. It is important to know if the sexual addict has sexual intercourse with someone that the details of the sexual positions are not necessary.

Results of Disclosure

What is effective disclosure?

The research study by Corley & Schneider (2002) of 80 sexual addicts and their partners asked the participants if they felt disclosure was an appropriate step for them. Sixty percent of addicts initially felt that disclosure was the proper course. Later in recovery, 96 percent of addicts felt disclosure was the right course of treatment for them. And on the same study, even with the pain and the trauma experienced, 81 percent of partners initially felt disclosure was the proper course of action and in later reflection, 96 percent felt that it was the right thing to do.[14]

What are the benefits of disclosure?

There is significant benefit for the spouse who finally hears the truth. The spouse is reminded that she did not imagine the acting-out behavior. With that knowledge comes empowerment. The partner is able to make healthy choices based on the truth.

Shameful behavior exposed to the light loses its power. The process helps sexual addicts "draw a line in the sand" from which they can move forward, living their lives free from compulsive sexual behavior. Disclosure has made it possible for the addict to share the most shameful secrets of the addictive past. This is an important step toward restoring personal integrity. The addict has discovered that he can tell the truth, even if the truth is not pleasant.

There are significant benefits for the relationship. Disclosure allows couples to move into a new relationship not dominated by secrets. This may be rare since it is likely that secrets exist in many relationships. Once the secrets are gone, the couple has the opportunity to develop true intimacy. Disclosure provides a foundation for continued recovery. It provides a base upon which trust and intimacy can be built.

To Separate or Not

Separation following disclosure may be necessary so a spouse can deal with feelings without pressure from the addict. In most cases, unless there is a threat or fear of physical violence, I strongly suggest that couples stay together. If the partner feels the need for space and time to process what has happened, I encourage the couple to live separately but in the same house.

In cases where the couple has young children, the separation may include sleeping in different beds in the same room. If the living situation allows, the couple can use separate rooms within the same house. Partners should have the option of deciding who will stay in which room. In some cases, the partner may ask the addict to move out temporarily. In that way, the partner has time to process feelings alone.

Some addicts are so dominating (verbally or physically) that the partner must get away from them temporarily or permanently. This is especially true where a sexual addict continues blaming his partner or puts pressure on her to immediately forgive or verbalize trust. If the partner decides to separate, I suggest she stay with a friend or family member rather than being alone. The support of a close friend is beneficial during a traumatic period.

If she needs a few days or more than a week to make sense of what she has heard in the disclosure, the partner should have the right to this time without any feelings of guilt. Separation should not be seen as a prelude to divorce.

Chapter 8

Polygraph Exams as an Aid to Recovery

Antonio's Story

Antonio, a consultant for a large computer company, failed his polygraph exam. He traveled several days each week. Sometimes he was gone for more than a week. His wife Joanne became suspicious after finding a receipt for flowers that she knows he did not purchase for her. He dismissed it by saying that it was not his receipt. When she pointed out that it was his credit card number and his name on the receipt, he went into a rage and told her it was "all in her head" and she was being paranoid.

Joanne hired a private investigator, whose report cited evidence that Antonio had been involved with several women in multiple cities. Soon afterward, Antonio and Joanne sought a sex addiction therapist.

Antonio worked diligently on his disclosure over several weeks. He indicated his desire to reveal all of his secrets. When the day of his disclosure came, he tearfully told his wife "everything" that he had done and went into detail about multiple relationships and how he had been deceptive.

However, when he took his polygraph exam, he failed on all counts. The questions ask him were rather standard, including the following one: "Is there anything else about your sexual activities that you haven't revealed to your wife?"

Antonio didn't reveal that one of the women he was sexual with was a work colleague. By withholding this secret Antonio, was not telling his wife the whole truth, failed the test, and lost Joanne's trust.

He felt he had good reason to withhold this detail: Antonio reasoned that since the affair had ended more than a year ago he did not want to risk his wife insisting that he make changes at work or perhaps change jobs.

His failure came from denying a fundamental truth: ***A disclosure that is less than 100 percent honest is not a disclosure but a deception!*** A person will have no difficulty passing the polygraph if he is completely honest and holds back nothing. Persons who withhold even the smallest detail do not have a chance of passing the exam.

Polygraph as an Aid

Polygraph exams are necessary to insure that true recovery is taking place. In drug treatment, a urinalysis is done at the beginning of treatment and randomly throughout treatment and aftercare. Drug treatment programs are ineffective without physical proof that the person remains drug free. Polygraph exams provide verification for a persons recovery from compulsive sexual behavior.

The successful sexual addict is an accomplished liar. Rather than a character attack, this statement acknowledges that the only way for an addict to hide his compulsive sexual behavior is to develop advanced skills at deception and duplicity. Sexual addicts can lie with such conviction that they may even convince themselves that the lies they tell are true. They lie with impunity and do it habitually and unconscious of how often they lie.

Deceptive behavior of sexual addicts is especially troublesome because some are so convincing that they can lie with tears in their eyes and tell their partners "This is the absolute truth." After repeatedly catching a sexual addict in a lie, the partner is left to wonder how to know the truth. Doubt undermines every aspect of a relationship, creating such insecurity that a wife may wonder, "Is he being truthful when he says he loves me?" Or when the husband of a wife who has repeatedly acted out hears her promise to be faithful, but remains skeptical.

Partial disclosures traumatize the partner. Polygraphs help get to the truth. Without this procedure many sexual addicts would never be able to tell the complete truth. Unless the hidden truth and accompanying shame are disclosed, the sexual addict may never be able to get free from an entrenched pattern of compulsive sexual behavior.

Sex addicts lie to their partners, therapists, and to themselves. A research project I conducted a few years ago among sexual addicts revealed with the clients were truthful about their behavior. A number of addicts said they had not been honest with their therapists about their behaviors.

One said, "I have lied through the years to all of my therapists. They are so gullible." Another admitted, "Therapists are so easy to fool. I just tell them what I think they want to hear." I accept I have been lied to in therapy in the past and will be lied to in the future.

I am not surprised that sexual addicts lie to their therapists, although it is disheartening that an addict would seek help for the addiction and then not be truthful about behavior. The nature of therapy requires a high level of trust with the client. Unless we are faced with information to the contrary or an implausible story, therapists are predisposed to believe what their clients say.

With the use of the polygraph I know the truth about clients' behaviors. As important, the spouses can be certain that the disclosure they receive in the clinical setting is complete. As one woman put it, "I can't trust my husband, but I can trust the polygraph exam!"

Does a spouse or partner have a right to know about the partner's sexual behavior?

Not only does she have a right but also the responsibility to know what the spouse or partner is involved in. Lying is a significant part of sexual addiction. Not only does deception keep one's spouse from finding out about the compulsive sexual behavior, it is often part of the defense mechanism addicts use to live with their addictive behaviors. Sexual addicts may lie to themselves about the impact of their behavior on their lives and their families. They may even have some success convincing themselves that they were justified in their sexual dalliances.

Polygraph exams expose the deception and lies. Not only does a polygraph exam allow spouses of sexual addicts to get to the truth, the exam requires addicts to bring to light the layers of shame that are keeping them enslaved to their addiction. Polygraph exams make it possible for them to finally tell the complete truth. Often this is the first time in his life that the sexual addict has been able to be totally truthful. It should be noted that while the decision to take a polygraph exam must rest with the addict, they have the opportunity to raise the level of credibility and accountability by following up disclosure with a polygraph exam.

Once sexual addicts realize that the polygraph exam is a tool for helping them get the whole truth out, they are able to be more forthright in their disclosure and expose all of the facts concerning their acting out. If a person is intent on being deceptive, polygraph exams expose this deception. Some may hold on to a secret with the hope that they can fool the polygraph examiner but fail their exam.

Today's polygraphs are highly reliable, computer-assisted tools for getting at the truth. False positives and other questionable outcomes are more a product of the outdated polygraph process rather than current practices.

What happens to those who fail a polygraph exam following a disclosure?

This indicates that they need to do additional work on their disclosure. What did they leave out? What did they remember but fail to write down? For the persons who say, "I have told everything that I remember" and they still fail, there is something they remember are holding back. Some secrets are buried so deeply or have such shame attached to them that it is extremely difficult for sexual addicts to tell them.

After working more on the disclosure, the sexual addict has an opportunity to take another polygraph exam. I have rarely seen an addict fail a second exam.

The typical polygraph protocol we use allows for four relevant questions that are supplied by the therapist in consultation with the spouse. These questions are developed in session with the couple present. Therefore the addict does not have any surprises about what is in the exam and the partner is able to make sure her concerns are addressed. The questions are global enough to cover the entire disclosure and specific enough to address areas of particular concern for the spouse.

The following are samples of questions that may be included on an initial polygraph exam. If other addictions are involved, at least one of the questions will relate to that addiction. Often a partner may want to have a question addressing a specific situation that the sexual addict has denied. The actual questions used will be determined after hearing the disclosure.

1. Is there anything about your sexual history you have not told your partner?
2. Was your disclosure a completely truthful description of your sexual behavior?
3. Do you have any other secrets you are keeping from your spouse?
4. Have you purposely omitted any sexual behavior from your disclosure?
5. Have you had physical sexual contact with any person other than what you have disclosed?
6. Have you intentionally viewed any pornography since _____?
7. Have you patronized sexually oriented business since _____?

As you can see, several questions are similar. Careful selection and wording of questions will reveal the truthfulness of the disclosure. Specificity is important. A greater concern is for the questions to be broad enough that they not allow some compulsive sexual behavior to go undetected. As a rule, we have several global questions and several specific questions.

Some spouses object to their partners knowing the questions that are going to be asked prior to the polygraph exam. They reason that they should not have time to prepare an answer. While this seems to be a valid point of view, giving the recovering addict the questions ahead of time does not give an unfair advantage for taking the exam. On the contrary, knowledge of the questions may help the individual see that the only way to pass the exam is to be completely truthful and allow for no omissions.

When the questions have been written, the addict goes to another office and takes the exam. He takes the disclosure along in case there are questions about behavior in his or her past. In the meanwhile, the partner and the partner's therapist have another individual session to further process the events of the formal disclosure. This additional therapy time is important because the spouse has been traumatized by what was disclosed and needs help to cope with what has transpired.

Additional information is often revealed during the polygraph exam. The reasons are that a sexual addict may have been holding back information hoping to slip this past the exam. This does not happen often. It is more likely that added pressure of taking the exam may cause the sexual addict to remember long hidden or forgotten secret or details.

What should the partner's response be in the sexual addict fails a polygraph exam?

The first response should be to reserve judgment. Realize that it is often a very difficult process for sexual addicts to stop a lifelong habit of lying and suddenly tell the whole truth. The belief that they may lose their relationship if they are candid about their behavior is a powerful incentive to hide the truth.

The partner can work with the sexual addict and the therapist in helping to create a safe place for the truth to be told, allowing for a foundation upon which trust can be built and the relationship can be put back on track.

If the addict fails a second polygraph exam, I encourage the partner to give him some additional latitude and continue working with the therapist to get the truth into the open. After work on the disclosure to uncover any details that have been hidden, we may seek out an alternative polygraph examiner to administer the subsequent exam. The goal is to help the addict to be completely honest and allow the partner to get to the truth. It is important for the partner to remember that this process is not to find a reason to get out of the relationship but rather to get to the complete truth.

What should the partner do if the addict refuses to take a polygraph exam or if he or she continues to take polygraph exams and fails with each attempt?

The partner needs to work with her therapist to determine what is in her best interest as well as the interest of any children who may be living at home. At this point some individuals, women in particular, experience a boundary collapse and decide that they want to hold on to the marriage at any cost even in the face of their spouse's continued deception and acting out. Whatever the choice, the partner should make decisions only after exploring all alternatives.

What if he or she fails the polygraph exam?

Parker's Story

Parker agreed to do a full disclosure to his partner Kacee. He also knew his therapist was going to encourage him to take a polygraph exam to verify that he had been truthful about his disclosure and had not omitted anything. The disclosure revealed many additional things that Kacee did not know and she was devastated by the information. When Parker took his polygraph exam, the questions focused on whether he had been truthful in the disclosure and whether he omitted any behavior. He failed the exam profoundly. When he swore he was telling the truth and that there must be some problem with the polygraph process, Kacee did not believe him. Parker was even tearful in pleading his case, pointing out that if he was going to intentionally lie that he would not have revealed many of the things that were included in the disclosure.

Parker's therapist was skilled in sex addiction therapy and did not use the failed test to badger Parker, but rather pointed out that it might be possible that there was either some event in his past that was so shameful that he could not bring himself to reveal it or there was a behavior that he felt Kacee would not be able to forgive. Parker committed to continue work with his therapist to see if there was something else in his background that he was either consciously or subconsciously holding back. After several sessions he finally told his therapist that there was one additional thing he had not revealed and that was a recent relationship he had with a fellow employee. He also felt that this last bit of information would cause Kacee to leave him. After revealing this last detail, Parker passed his polygraph exam verifying that there were no other hidden behaviors. Ultimately Parker and Kacee stayed together but he opted to get a job with a different company.

There are several reasons a person may fail a polygraph exam. One reason which must be dealt with up front is the margin of error that is inherent in all diagnostic processes, such as medical exams. Current polygraph exams have a 94%+ accuracy rate. Sexual addicts who fail exams are often quick to suggest that they are truthful and that the exams are inaccurate. After doing additional therapy, if the client maintains there is nothing new to disclose, I offer then the opportunity to take another exam and even offer the opportunity to use another examiner.

They passed the polygraph exam: Now what?
Passing their polygraph exams following disclosure, is such a momentous event for sex addicts that they often feel as if they should be congratulated for telling the truth. Certainly, it is a laudable accomplishment for them to be able to make a break with their long-standing habit of telling lies and to finally reveal the complete truth about their behavior. During the next several days after passing

polygraph exam, the partner may want to express appreciation for the addict telling the truth and perhaps for the courage to take that step. But the exuberant behavior of the sexual addict may well be a stark contrast to the anger or sadness that the partner feels after learning the details from the disclosure. The partner should allow himself the freedom to feel a full range of emotions and express them to the addict. The best place to do this is in a clinical setting with the therapist present. The partner must have the opportunity to express whatever emotion is felt.

The spouse's therapist will help him or her to understand the importance of expressing his emotions and the addict's therapist will help the sexual addict listen without retreating into shame. It is appropriate for the addict to feel guilt over the acting-out behavior but it is not helpful to plunge into shame. Guilt is awareness that he or she did some things that were wrong. Shame is the sexual addict seeing himself or herself as a bad person.

Following the polygraph exam, the couple and both therapists reconvene for the polygraph report session. In some cases there are additional details that have come to light and these will need to be talked about at length. Many times no additional details are revealed. When this is the case the report session becomes anticlimactic, but this is still an important component in the process. After the polygraph exam the disclosure is shredded. If it was prepared on a computer, the sexual addict is encouraged to delete the file, because continuing to revisit the disclosure document is re-traumatizing to the partner.

Misuse of Polygraph Exams

Polygraph exams should be used as a part of recovery only if they are an integrated part of therapy. Great harm has been done when a couple has engaged a polygraph examiner directly without utilizing the services of a trained sex addiction therapist familiar with integrating polygraph into the therapeutic process.

There have been cases where additional acting out and secrets were revealed after a person had taken and passed a polygraph exam somewhere else. In each case, the previous exams that were administered did not follow a clinical disclosure but rather asked non-specific questions about their sexual behavior. The false assurance given by an erroneous exam impedes sexual addiction recovery because the addict still has secrets that will likely lead them back into their addiction.

The person being tested should not be treated as a criminal. Polygraph exams should not be used in a punitive way or as a way of "getting the goods" on someone suspected of being unfaithful. For that reason it requires that the therapist work closely with the polygraph examiner and develop a procedure that treats the addict with the utmost respect and does not have any of the overtones of a criminal procedure. Polygraph exams that are part of sexual addiction recovery therapy are used as an aid to the addict to help strip away all of the layers of deception that have been used to facilitate the addiction.

If a sexual addict really believes his partner will leave him, he will be likely to try to protect secrets as long as possible. The fact that he is engaged in sexual addiction therapy that includes a disclosure and polygraph is evidence that he wants to get rid of all of his secrets. It takes a patient and a supportive therapist to guide this difficult process, even if it means doing additional disclosure and a follow-up test after failing the first polygraph exam. An initial exam failure is not final for the individual. Instead this is an indication that further work must to be done to get to the bottom of the secrets so that the addict can finally become free.

It is tempting for some couples to use polygraph exams for settling arguments or validating an assertion of the sexual addict. They may say, "I can prove to you that I'm telling the truth. I'll go take a polygraph exam!" Or the partner may exclaim, "I don't believe you. You need to take a polygraph exam."

To use polygraph in this way is misuse of a valuable tool. It is also a misuse of polygraph exams at the beginning of recovery to "get the goods" on the sexual addict to determine whether the partner wants to stay in the marriage. Polygraph exams are helpful for verifying a clinically controlled and orchestrated disclosure and for monitoring continued progress in recovery. Couples should resist the urge to use the polygraph capriciously or punitively. Instead, the couple should be content with a previously agreed-upon schedule for follow-up exams.

Chapter 9

Celibacy Contract

Julius' Story

Julius first saw pornography at age thirteen when visiting at the home of a friend. He was shown a collection of magazines that were filled with photos of naked women. Julius experienced a strong emotional reaction from viewing the first photo. From then on he would seize any opportunity to get another look at those magazines.

He would often suggest to his friend that they look at the explicit magazines. Julius recalled his friend reacting negatively and complaining that all he wanted to do was look at those magazines. As Julius grew older, he slowly gathered his own collection of pornography. From that time on he was never without a stash of porn.

As an adult, he had bookmarked hundreds of websites where he could view pornography. He spent five hours or more each evening searching for new sites. His search was not just for any pornography but for certain types of photos. When he found photos that he liked he would download them and store them on his computer. He would continue the search for the perfect photos that fit the profile of his ideal fantasy partner. Julius has downloaded hundreds of thousands of photos and videos and has spent an average of over thirty hours each week on his cybersex behavior. By his own estimation he has spent over eight thousand hours engaged in his sexual addiction in just five years. He has realized that he invested time in his addiction that was almost equal to having another full-time job.

At the suggestion of his therapist, Julius and his partner decided to write a celibacy contract. His therapist told Julius that he believed a period of celibacy would help him to clear his mind of the many pornography images that he had seen and help set the stage for later moving into healthy sexuality with his partner. With the establishment of the initial contract period, Julius and his partner were encouraged to see the contract as part of the treatment process and not as punishment.

Celibacy Contract

As the name suggests, a celibacy contract is an agreement between the couple to forgo all sexual activities for a period of time. Typical contracts are set for thirty days and then reviewed with the couple with possible extensions made on a monthly basis. There are several advantages to a celibacy contract. The first is that it removes the "drug of choice" from a sexual addict.

Sexual addiction is a dependence on the release of the naturally-occurring chemicals in the brain knows as neurotransmitters. A first step in treating drug or alcohol abuse is to take the addict completely off his drug so that treatment can begin in earnest. A celibacy contract has the effect of taking the sexual addict off his or her "drug".

The celibacy contract will preclude not only sexual intercourse between the couple but all sexual activity. It should also include a ban on all masturbation, use of pornography, and any other sexual behavior involving other people or self. If masturbation does not end, the celibacy contract is of no practical benefit.

Compulsive sexual behavior is used as a drug to take away pain, to cope with stress, to manage difficult circumstances in life, and perhaps even as a reward for some achievement. When sex is removed, addicts often have a variety of feelings and emotions surface that are unfamiliar to them since they usually medicate themselves to keep from feeling them. During a celibacy contract, addicts have a chance to get in touch with their feelings and face what they have been hiding.

It is important that both partners are in therapy as often as twice a week for the duration of the celibacy contract so that they are able to process feelings and emotions that may be coming to the surface. Sometimes the issues that surface during this period provide significant insight into the treatment of the compulsive sexual behavior. If sex has been used to solve problems or end disagreements in the relationship, the contract period will encourage couples to deal with their difficulties more directly.

The mention of a celibacy contract often brings fear to an addict. I have heard individuals, particularly men, say that they cannot even conceive of going a week without sex, to say nothing of a month or longer. If they are that dependent on sex, the celibacy contract will allow them to face some of the fears they have associated with a temporary abstinence.

Partners often greet the thought of a celibacy contract with a sense of relief. In some relationships partners feel pressured to be sexual at a frequency that is far beyond their comfort zone. Also, they may dread sex because it is often one-sided with the sexual addict's appetite being the first priority and the partner's needs being marginalized.

There are several advantages to a celibacy contract. As has been mentioned earlier, it allows for the examination of feelings that may have been masked by sex. Another advantage to a celibacy contract is that it allows the couple to develop a healthy sexual appetite for each other. This is especially helpful in relationships where the husband does not seem to have much interest in sex with his wife. If he completely ends his sexual behavior, including all masturbation and pornography use, his sexual appetite has an opportunity to normalize, hopefully resulting in a greater desire to have sex with his wife. This normalization process often requires the contract be extended to 60 to 90 days or more. This may seem like an eternity, but the renewed intimacy that can result is worth the wait.

Another advantage to a celibacy contract is that the period of sexual abstinence provides time for a couple to consider what kind of sexual relationship they want to maintain. If the relationship has included activities that either partner believes were unhealthy or made them uncomfortable, this is a good time to eliminate them from their sexual repertory. Healthy sexuality includes only those sexual acts that are mutually consensual. A period of celibacy allows time for reflection on the entire sexual relationship.

It is common to the human condition for all of us to yearn for intimacy in our committed relationships. Yet for the sexual addict, because he or she frequently divorces emotion from sex, he often substitutes intensity for intimacy. Healthy sexual relationships may indeed have times of great intensity. But a defined period of celibacy allows couples to carefully examine their sexual relationship and choose to have it defined by true intimacy rather than intensity.

Celibacy contracts are often started at the beginning of recovery. It should be stressed that it is best to enter into these contracts under a therapist's supervision. And since such contracts frequently take place prior to a formal disclosure the partner does not know whether or not the sexual addict partner has been sexual with other persons. Regardless if the acting-out behavior was that of the husband or the wife, this is a good time for both to have tests for sexually-transmitted diseases. For the sake of health the partner must assume there is a possibility they have been exposed to STDs.

For many couples, a celibacy contract is entered into while they are working toward disclosure. This is a period when the partner typically experiences a mixture of feelings as the spouse or companion waits for the addict to give details about acting-out behaviors. The partner is relieved from any pressure to perform sexually at a time when he or she feels most vulnerable. This is also a time when the addict can focus on exploring all of his or her acting-out behavior in preparation for the disclosure and not use sex to medicate any feelings that may have been stirred up.

Celibacy Contract

Sexual Addict's Commitment

As part of my ongoing recovery, I have admitted to myself that I have become powerless over my sexual behavior. In order to strengthen my resolve and conditions for my recovery, I agree to abide by the conditions of this contract. I will refrain from engaging in:

- Sexual behavior of any kind. (This includes sexual or sensual touch and open mouth kisses.)
- Appearing nude or semi-clothed (exhibitionism).
- Masturbation.
- All seductive behavior.
- Pornography (Internet, print, or video).
- All sexual conversations or suggestive innuendos.
- I will report sexual fantasizing to my therapist, my weekly 12-step group, my sponsor, and my weekly therapy group with the desire of gaining support as I maintain this celibacy period.

The purpose of this contract is to help prevent sexually dependent behaviors, cope with fantasy, and aid my return to healthy sexuality.

Adherence to this contract may result in recall of many childhood memories. Anxiety will probably increase, as I will be unable to use my sexual behavior as a coping mechanism.

My groups, my therapist and my sponsor need to be aware of my celibacy contract so that they can be of support to me.

Spouse's/Partner's Commitment

As the spouse/partner of a man or woman who is in treatment for compulsive sexual behavior, I realize I have a responsibility to support my partner in this celibacy contract. For the duration of the contract period, I pledge to do the following:

- Not engage in sexual behavior of any kind with my partner.
- Not engage in any seductive behavior with my partner.
- Do all within my power to support my partner's desire to remain celibate for the duration of this contract period.
- Report any attempts made by my partner to be sexual or seductive.

This contract is in effect for _____ days starting today,

_____,

(Check up sessions will be scheduled with the couple every 30 days during the contract period.)

This contract is scheduled to be reviewed _____

_____. However, the contract will only end when unanimously agreed upon between the husband, the wife, and the therapist during a therapy session.

(Prior to the expiration of this contract, the therapist will prepare the couple for resuming their sexual relationship with each other.)

Client Signature:

_____ Date: ____/____/____

Spouse/Partner Signature:

_____ Date: ____/____/____

Therapist Signature:

_____ Date: ____/____/____

The celibacy contract is used at Hope & Freedom Counseling. Although this contract addresses most of the addict's behaviors, conditions specific to a particular marriage or long-term relationship can be added.

A celibacy contract takes cooperation of both partners. Not only must the addict have a commitment to refrain from all sexual activity, the spouse or partner also needs to be willing to give up sex for a defined period of time. This may be frightening to the partner of an addict because of her fear the spouse or partner will search for sexual release somewhere else if the addict does not have a sexual outlet at home. But it is important for the partners to remain firm and not resort to seductive behavior, which some individuals do when they wonder if their partner still finds them attractive. It is a painful period that must be endured. Yet to help the addict and strengthen the relationship of both members, celibacy must be maintained.

The couple is prepared for the period of celibacy through education as to its benefits and to the fact that celibacy is temporary. It is equally important that consideration be given as to how to end the celibacy contract. The couple is told that the contract can only come to an end during a therapy session when it is unanimously agreed to by the husband, the wife, and the therapist. If the wife or husband is seeing a different therapist, it is important that both therapists be in agreement for the contract to end.

In restarting the sexual relationship, there is value in encouraging the couple to continue to abstain from sexual intercourse for the first several sexual encounters. The emphasis should be on getting to know each other better and on providing pleasure for each other. Often the elimination of any expectation of intercourse will allow the couple to grow in their appreciation of each other and eliminate any performance anxiety that may accompany the end of the celibacy period.

Chapter 10

The Partner's Recovery Journey

The sexual addict tells his partner that things are all in her mind or she is crazy, or even that she should be ashamed of her suspicion. The partner usually has an intuition that something is wrong. Sometimes there is no reason to be suspicious. Sometimes suspicions result from active imagination or projection of one's fear that the current partner is at unfaithful as a previous partner was, or the result of watching too many TV and movie melodramas. Sometimes, though, suspicions are well-founded. I have talked to a number of individuals who said that their partners or spouses were so believable that they succeeded in convincing them that perhaps they were imagining that there was a problem. The result of being told "you're just imagining things" for years is that some people learn to dismiss their inner voice that tells them something is truly wrong. The place to begin is to focus on what is known. Start with the following list of questions and ask if any of them fit your partner. However, don't jump to conclusions. There are legitimate reasons why a person may have one or several of these behaviors.

Behaviors surrounding the suspected sexual addict's work:
- Has your partner stayed after work a lot and been unable to adequately explain why?
- Does your partner have to work on the weekends now but that has not been required to in the past?
- When staying at work late, is your partner is not available by phone?

- Has the number of your partner's business trips increased without explanation?
- When you offer to accompany her on a business trip did your partner find excuses why that wouldn't be a good idea?
- Does your partner describe a relationship with a co-worker as being "just friends?"

Behaviors surrounding appearance:
- Has your partner started dressing better?
- Has your partner started working out, losing weight, getting his or her hair colored, abruptly started using cologne or perfume and started focusing more attention on personal appearance?
- Does your partner keep an extra change of clothes in the car or at work without a plausible explanation?
- Has your spouse left the house wearing one outfit and come home dressed differently?
- Does your partner smell fresh and clean (as if he just showered or used cologne or perfume) at the end of the day?
- Has your partner inexplicably laundered clothes or dropped off a single piece of clothing at the dry cleaners?

Behaviors surrounding phone use:
- Does your partner often not answer the cell phone when you call?
- Does your partner sometimes not answer his cell phone when with you? (Perhaps your partner looks at the screen and then says the call is not important.)
- Does your partner try to end cell phone calls hurriedly when you are around?
- Has your partner started sending and receiving text messages when that has not been part of the pattern of communication?

- Does your partner get phone calls that have to be taken in private? (Certainly there are appropriate times when privacy is necessary. But an unexplained need for privacy causes suspicion.)
- Has your partner purchased a "calling card" for no apparent reason?
- Have you discovered that your partner has purchased an additional cell phone that is kept in a secret place or is left at work?
- When your phone rings at home, do the persons calling often hang up when you answer?
- When your spouse or partner answers the phone, does your partner frequently say, "You have the wrong number," and then hang up?
- Does your partner erase text messages or the record of calls made or received?

Behaviors surrounding pagers and Blackberries:
- Has your partner recently acquired a pager and become secretive about its use?
- Have you noticed that when your partner's pager goes off there is a random display of numbers that don't make sense? (Some persons have used prearranged codes with a sex partner to identify the time or place for a rendezvous. This can also be true with text messages.)
- Has your partner acquired a Blackberry or some other device that allows her to be in constant email contact but not have a plausible explanation for why she needs the device?

Behaviors surrounding your communication:
- Does it seem that you and your partner are having arguments more frequently, sometimes followed by his leaving?
- Has your partner started questioning your daily schedule more frequently?
- Have you caught your partner in lies both large and small?

Behaviors surrounding his use of time:

- Is your partner frequently unavailable for family outings and activities?
- Are there periods of time when your spouse or partner cannot account for his or her whereabouts?
- Does your partner get defensive if you ask about his or her schedule or erratic behavior?
- Does your partner get angry if you ask where he has been?

Behaviors surrounding money:

- Has your partner started using cash for daily purchases rather than using credit cards or checks?
- Are there numerous cash withdrawals (for banks or ATMs) that your partner cannot adequately explain?
- Has gasoline usage suddenly grown greater than normal?
- Are there gasoline purchases at stations that are well outside of your partner's normal traffic pattern?
- Does your partner get irritated when you ask questions about the family finances?
- Have you discovered a secret account, credit card, money or stash?
- Does your partner have unexplained credit card charges?
- Does your partner take company expense reimbursements in cash?
- Has your partner recently moved significant sums of money from an account but not been able to give you a good reason for the move?
- Has your partner made decisions with your family finances that seems reckless or irresponsible, like closing accounts, removing your name from accounts, taking out loans, or changing the way retirement accounts are set up?

Behaviors surrounding computer use:

- Does your spouse or partner use suggestive screen names when he gets on the Internet?

- If you enter the room and your partner is working on the computer, does she hurriedly close a program or make some quick movement to keep you from seeing what is on the screen?
- Have you noticed an increase in pornographic "spam" email on your home computer?
- Has the history in your Internet browser been erased?
- Have you found pornographic images on your home computer?
- Has your spouse or partner purchased a web cam, scanner, or digital camera for what seems like a contrived reason, or tried to convince you of the need to make such a purchase?
- Does your partner get up in the middle of the night, saying he cannot sleep then starts working on the computer?
- Have you previously caught him looking at pornography or being involved in some other cybersex activity and each time he has promises to stop, but the behavior continues?

Behaviors surrounding sexual behavior:
- Has your partner's sexual appetites changed recently?
- Is your partner suddenly more interested in sex than in the past?
- Has your partner's sexual appetite diminished significantly?
- Has your partner started using new sexual moves or positions?
- Has your partner started to pressure you to do some things sexually with which you are not comfortable?
- Has your partner asked you to go to a sexually-oriented or "adult" business when that has not been part of your past practice?
- Has your partner abruptly adopted a rigid, judgmental attitude about persons who engage in behavior that she would consider unacceptable? (This attitude may or may not concern some sexual behavior.)

The presence of any one or even several of these things is not proof that there is a problem. You are in a discovery process and the preceding questions simply serve to guide that process. If you are noticing things that seem unusual, they may or may not be anything to be concerned about.

Sexual addicts can be clever and cunning. While I do not recommend the procedure, some hire private investigator to find out if their suspicions have any foundation. Sometimes they learn that their companion has not been doing anything that would be considered inappropriate. Other times they find out that their partner's unexplained absences or financial expenditures were the result of innocent behavior.

But there are occasions when the investigator provides irrefutable proof that a partner has been acting out sexually. Such proof is often devastating. But it may also be affirming to know that you were not being unreasonably suspicious.

There are countless stories of individuals who have found a stash of pornographic photos on the family computer or found the Internet history shows that numerous pornography websites have been visited. Women have found receipts to sexual massage parlors or strip clubs, seen their partner sneak out of a neighbor's house in the middle of the day, or have observed some other behavior that cannot easily be explained away. Women, too, have conducted extensive sexual relationships over the Internet, and, in other cases, carried out extramarital affairs.

Be certain not to let suspicious behavior cloud your thinking so that you make a leap and call suspicions fact. But if you do have proof your spouse or partner has been involved in compulsive sexual behavior, you are faced with a choice: What do you do with what you now know?

Confrontation and Intervention

What do you do once you know for certain your partner is involved in compulsive sexual behavior? You can choose to ignore it. Perhaps that is what you have done in the past. Have you had proof of past indiscretions and dismissed them with the hope that they were one-time anomalies? Maybe you convinced yourself that if you didn't confront your partner with what you knew that things would get better.

If you have practiced denial in the past, has that worked for you? The fact that you are reading this book indicates that it did not have the desired result.

Ignoring the problem will not make it go away. If your partner is an addict, your partner will not outgrow his addiction. The only remaining options are:

Terminate the relationship. Decide you have had enough and that your partner probably cannot change. End the relationship and try to put the pieces of your life back together.

or

Fight for your relationship and insist that your partner get immediate help to permanently stop the mutually-destructive acting out.

The second option is not the same as giving a second chance. This option calls for you to determine that you are not going to go on living with a person who continues to act out sexually. No excuse is satisfactory for past behavior. The fact that your partner is a sexual addict does not relieve the responsibility for the actions in the past or present. The recovering sexual addict must take responsibility for what was done to you and your relationship. Most immediately, he or she must be willing to seek professional help.

When confronted with their behavior, some sexual addicts continue to lie and deny that they have done anything sexually inappropriate. Others try to minimize their behavior by saying that

"All men do it," or "It's just a guy thing," or "I just chatted with other men, I never met any in person," or even "I'm a sexual addict and I can't help it." They may respond with denials, anger, minimizing, rationalizing, or doing any number of other things to try to escape responsibility for their actions.

You Are Not Crazy!

In spite of what an addict tells you, you are not crazy. By this time you have found out that your suspicions are not all in your mind. When you first became apprehensive of your partner's behavior, all you may have known was that things did not add up. Your partner would say that he was working late and at first you believed the excuse.

But when your suspicions grew greater and you mentioned your concerns, your partner dismissed you by saying that you were imagining things or that it was "all in your head." Your partner may even have shamed you for your feelings or made fun of you.

You might have noticed that money was missing and been told that it got lost or misplaced. Perhaps your partner even blamed things on you and attempted to make you to feel like you could not trust your memory. You began to second-guess yourself. You may have even started to believe that it was all in your head. Some individuals even buy books about how they can cope with their memory loss because their spouse or partner convinced them that they must be suffering from Alzheimer's disease.

But then you get your first solid proof that there is something untoward going on. Your spouse is seen with another woman or man and does not have an adequate explanation. Or maybe you overheard a phone conversation and discovered that he was setting up a secret rendezvous.

Now you know. You are not imagining it! You finally know that your partner has been deceiving you.

It is normal for women and men to go through all of the stages of grief as they try to come to terms with their feelings. You have worked through denial and now you have to deal with your anger over your partner's behavior. You are livid, and why shouldn't you be? It isn't fair. It isn't just. He has hurt you and has disregarded your feelings. Perhaps your partner has even put your health at risk by having sex with other people.

Mixed with the anger is sadness that seems to overwhelm you. You may feel that you are being swallowed up by grief. Nothing you do takes away the pain that you feel. And, you do not feel that you can talk to anyone about what is going on. There may not be anyone who you feel will understand and will also be able to keep your confidence.

A portion of your sadness may be in wondering why your spouse or partner is not satisfied to keep your sexual relationship exclusive. He or she may have even said things to you that have caused you to believe that you are inadequate, especially sexually. The sexual addict may be heaping shame and guilt on you by pronouncing you as the reason he is seeking sex elsewhere. The problem is not with you. The sexual addict is the one who has the problem. His behavior is the result of the addiction, and not you.

Do not give in to the attack. Maintain your boundaries.

No matter how much you comply sexually, you are not going to cure his sexual addiction. If you give in to his sexual demands your partner will continue to indulge in compulsive behavior and only result in dragging you into his insanity.

Set Healthy Boundaries

This section is not meant to help you examine your past and future boundaries.

The first boundary to consider is if it is acceptable to be in a relationship with a person who continues to act out sexually. If that it is not acceptable, then you are on your way to setting one of your most important boundaries. When you set boundaries, you must determine how you are going to maintain those boundaries and what the consequences will be if they are violated.

If you determine that you are not going to be in relationship with an individual who continues acts out sexually, then you must tell your partner. You may prefer to do this in the presence of a friend or therapist for support. Avowing your boundaries is not the same as saying you are not going to remain in a relationship with a sexual addict. Sexual addiction is treatable and responds very favorably to a combination of therapy and work in 12-step fellowships.

If you are setting boundaries it is important to work out ahead of time the full ramifications of establishing boundaries with your support system. What are you prepared to do to back up this decision? Are you so certain of this decision and willing to walk away from the relationship if your spouse or partner does not get into recovery?

This is one of the most difficult decisions that you will make.

Contemplating Life on Your Own

It is often frightening to consider separation. You are not looking for reasons to get out of your relationship. However, unless you take a stand that you will not remain in a relationship with your partner continuing to be sexual outside of your relationship, your partner may never stop acting out.

Contemplating life on your own is not the same as making an empty threat. Rather you are preparing to enforce your boundary not to be in a relationship unless love and sex are reserved exclusively for your relationship. Are you emotionally ready to take this stand?

A good exercise for you is to keep a journal about various life situations and consider how you will handle them as a single person. If you have children, what will it be like raising them by yourself? How will you address all of the concerns, from childcare to health insurance to transportation – not to mention housing and food – by yourself?

Healthy boundaries dictate that you have enough respect for yourself to determine that you will not remain in a relationship with a person unwilling to live in a monogamous relationship with you.

The only way to back up that boundary is to be financially able to care for yourself in the event that the relationship ends.

Are you financially ready to consider life on your own? Do you have the financial resources necessary to address the many concerns you will face if you are on your own? Do you have a job or career that will provide the on-going financial support you need if you and your partner end your relationship? If you do not have a job or a career, you will need a plan for life on your own.

I am not advocating divorce without careful consideration and discussion. It is painful to admit and realize if your spouse refuses to address his sexual behavior and enter recovery, your relationship will become more difficult to maintain.

Regardless of your partner's situation you need to contemplate life without your partner. Do not misunderstand this to mean that you need to end your relationship. You need to decide what to do if the relationship ends and there will be a number of legal concerns.

Protect Yourself!

It is imperative to protect yourself in the event your marriage or relationship ends. If you have confronted your partner over the sexual behavior and he is not willing to seek help, you need to make sure to look out for your interests and those of your children. Be alert for signs of suspicious activities with your assets. Has he or she opened additional accounts or made transfers that do not make sense? Do not sign anything regarding a financial transaction or a change in your business if you suspect your partner is hiding things from you. You may need an attorney. This is not the prelude to a divorce. It is a preemptive move to protect your interests. You must not wait until assets have been moved and documentation hidden.

Such actions may seem like an over-reaction. It is possible that your partner is not doing anything wrong with the family assets, but if you see indications of this, it is in your interest to protect yourself.

After going through these steps and preparing for life on your own, you are ready to confront your partner with an ultimatum.

Don't be surprised if your partner says, "Fine, if that's the way you want it, then we can just live apart."

You may be tested to see if you will back down. There is a good chance that your partner may believe he wants to be single. That is a choice he will have to make. Before you capitulate, consider this: with no boundary to maintain, he may never enter recovery. Why should your partner change while enjoying the benefits of your relationship and continuing compulsive sexual behavior at the same time?

Are you so desperate that you will keep your partner under any circumstances? Or, to regain your self-respect will you insist that the only way for you to stay in the relationship is for your partner to stop all of the extra-curricular sexual activity and do concentrated work in recovery? Is it better to have a spouse who cheats and will not tell the truth? Or is better to have integrity and an exclusive relationship? No one else can make these decisions for you. But once you make them, you will gain strength.

Your boundaries do not determine your partner's behavior. They announce your confidence as a person who does not have to settle for an unfaithful partner. You deserve more, and only you can stand up for yourself and say, "Unfaithfulness ends today!"

The Wounded You: Dealing With Your Trauma

Janelle's Story

Janelle has been in recovery for five years following the revelation that her husband Tobey was a sex addict. She worked hard and learned how to set healthy boundaries for herself. The first 18 months after the discovery of her husband's compulsive sexual behavior were very difficult. They continued to make progress and her husband was into solid recovery and successful in stopping all acting-out behavior.

They sought the help of skilled therapists who understood sexual addiction. Recovery progressed well. Trust was slowly rebuilt over the years to the point that they had a much better relationship than before the discovery of his sexual addiction. Janelle believed she was completely healed of the trauma she suffered. It had been years since she worried that Tobey would act out again. She was no longer troubled by the thoughts.

What has surprised Janelle is that a couple of times lately she found herself getting profoundly sad as she thought about the early years of their marriage. Once she even dissolved into tears when a scene from a movie reminded her of the past. She immediately went back to her therapist and restarted her individual therapy.

After several sessions her therapist concluded that Janelle had indeed largely healed from the trauma. The therapist also helped her to realize that while the trauma wound had healed, a tender scar that remained. Although she had some sadness about the past, that sorrow was not an indicator that she was not doing well or had not done significant healing. Janelle realized that some of the impact of Tobey's acting-out would continue to affect her in spite of the strong recovery they had.

Following disclosure and a successful polygraph exam, sexual addicts often feel relief. They finally have gotten out secrets that they would have not divulged. Perhaps they have a sense of satisfaction or pride. They have finally told the truth. They may be looking for their partners to applaud their truth-telling and tell them how proud they are to be in the relationship.

Partners may feel relief for knowing the truth and also sadness and anger about what they learned. Some are traumatized like survivors of war or seeing a violent death, or living through a horrible natural disaster. Trauma may continue for years after the sexual addict has achieved sobriety.

Several research studies have added insights about what the partners of sexual addicts suffer following disclosure—that they are victims of trauma. A study by Dr. Jennifer Schneider during 2000 found that following disclosure, the spouse felt hurt, betrayal, rejection, abandonment, devastation, loneliness, shame, isolation, humiliation, jealousy, and anger as well as loss of self-esteem.

The most startling finding is that disclosure may propagate the features of post-traumatic stress disorder, or PTSD. In 2004, Coop-Gordon, Baucom and Snyder found high levels of PTSD symptoms among partners within the first year following disclosure or discovery of an extra-marital affair.[18] A study by Steffens & Rennie in 2006 found 69.9 percent of participants met all but one criteria for diagnosis of PTSD using a tool known as the Post traumatic stress Diagnostic Scale (PDS). They also found that 71.7 percent demonstrated a severe level of functional impairment in major areas of their lives as measured by the PDS.[19]

"I feel like I have just been kicked in the chest!" one man remarked after his partner's disclosure. "Why do I hurt so much?" said a wife after disclosure. Variations of this statement are often made when spouses discover they are married to a sexual addict. You may have feelings of sadness or anger. Perhaps the initial anger has been worked through but there is still have a terrible feeling in the pit of your stomach. What is going on? These are the effects of trauma.

For several decades, mental health professionals have come to expect that persons who have been at war, in a terrible accident, or witnessed a horrible atrocity will suffer from aftereffects of trauma. During World War I, this was called "shell shock." Doctors noticed that patients might have early symptoms of irritability, tiredness, lack of concentration, or headaches. Some suffered from panic attacks and deserted. The doctors concluded that soldiers were suffering from the aftereffects of artillery shells exploding near them. It was theorized that the exploding shells created a vacuum that upset the cerebral-spinal fluid and upset the working of the brain.

This disorder has also been called "combat stress" and even "war neurosis." But it was found that a person didn't have to be in war to suffer some of the same symptoms. People who survived natural disasters, terrible accidents, or an act of great violence could also suffer in the same way. Shell shock and combat stress designations were replaced with a Post-Traumatic Stress Disorder or PTSD during the 1980s.

PTSD is a neurological injury and not a mental illness. PTSD is a natural reaction to some unnatural situation. Historically, a criterion for diagnosing PTSD was the existence of a single major life-threatening event. Today there is growing recognition that PTSD may be caused by an accumulation of smaller events that, by themselves, are not life threatening. However, most of the mental health community still looks for the major life-threatening event to aid in their diagnosis of PTSD.

Does this relate to you? Have you been traumatized by revelations that your partner is a sexual addict? In fact, you may have had multiple revelations through the years that have added to the total weight of the trauma that is impacting you.

Other symptoms of PTSD may include flashbacks of traumatizing events, feelings of intense fear or helplessness, decreased interest or participation in important activities, or perhaps an inability to recall an important aspect of the trauma. Some persons suffering from PTSD report feelings of detachment or an inability to express loving feelings for their partner. Outbursts of anger, difficulty concentrating, and sleep disturbances are also common. Some develop an exaggerated startle-response and others may become hyper-vigilant.

There are effective treatments for PTSD. A researched non-medical psychotherapeutic technique that targets PTSD is Eye Movement Desensitization and Reprocessing, or EMDR. This therapy helps process the troublesome memories and events to relieve PTSD.[20] In addition to EMDR, individual and group therapy using cognitive-behavioral techniques may treat PTSD. Sometimes psychotropic drugs may be helpful in treating PTSD. These are useful as long as the client is able to come to terms with the traumatic events. The most important first step is to see a therapist skilled working with the partners of sexual addicts and have an assessment and evaluation.

Following disclosure, it is important for the addict to learn how to properly respond while the partner works through the particular trauma. The recovering sexual addict will be taught to validate the partner during the potentially lengthy time that he or she is dealing with the trauma. Unless the partner is allowed to express anger and process the full range of feelings, healing will not occur.

The discovery of your partner's acting out has had a significant traumatic impact. Do not expect a quick resolution to that trauma. You may require therapy for two or more years. The healing from your pain is a lengthy process If you have experienced sexual or physical abuse in addition to the emotional abuse from your spouse or partner, you may need more extensive therapy to deal with underlying issues.

The greater the trauma endured, the greater the need for you to be active in organizations like Co-SA or other 12-step fellowships that support partners of sexual addicts. Therapy and 12-step meeting attendance are crucial to healing. The support network you build in these meetings will help to sustain you between therapy sessions and help make sense out of the insanity of addiction.

While the addiction is the addict's, you have been injured by it and need attention to your own healing. Treat yourself kindly and begin your own recovery even if your spouse or partner is not in recovery.

There are helpful books for the partners of sexual addicts listed in the appendix. One of the most helpful is *Through the Trauma Lens*, by Marsha Means and Barbara Steffens.

Dealing With Your Own Pain

"My spouse is doing well in recovery. Why can't I get on with my life?" I hear this frequently from spouses and partners of sexual addicts. The answer is elusive. There may be a number of factors at work. The heart of the difficulty is that partners have been traumatized by the discovery or disclosure of the sexual acting out. Frequently, partners ask, "My spouse has begged me for a second chance. Should I grant it?" In some relationships, it is not a second chance that the addict asks for but a third, fourth, tenth, or hundredth chance.

The answer must come from you. Do you believe your partner's sincerity enough to continue being with this person in spite of the regressions? Is your partner engaged in a robust program of recovery that includes 12-step meetings, working with a sponsor, and therapy? It is not enough to hear the words that they are going to change. You have a right to expect to see a change in behavior and significant recovery activities. No matter what decision you make, you must make care of yourself. Consider engaging in individual therapy or couples therapy. Determine what behavior is acceptable and what is not for you. If you accept some behavior (even if it is "just porn"), you can expect acting out to continue. For whatever is unacceptable, set the boundary and hold firm.

Chapter 11

Slip and Relapse Recovery

Freeman's Story

Freeman started his acting out long before the inception of the Internet. As a young teenager, Freeman found his first soft pornographic "men's magazines" in a dumpster. When he was a freshman in high school a friend brought a nudist magazine to school. He traded his bicycle for the magazine since it was the first time he had ever seen a photo of a nude woman. Freeman was captivated by what he saw.

As a young adult, he gathered every pornographic magazine he could find. Gradually, he started seeking hard-core pornography but did not like having to go to the adult bookstores. With the advent of the Internet, he could find what he wanted on the computer. By the time he got into recovery, Freeman was spending a good portion of each day looking at pornography at work. He was terrified when he heard that his company had installed software to determine which employees were violating the company computer policies.

After reading about sexual addiction on the Internet, Freeman entered recovery. He attended 12-step meetings, got a sponsor and worked the steps. Gradually Freeman decreased his meeting attendance and stopped meeting with his sponsor. He reasoned that since he had gone several months without acting out that he was probably cured and did not need to continue his recovery activities.

Months later, Freeman had his first slip. He clicked on an Internet news story about the arrest of a celebrity. Two clicks later he was viewing hardcore pornography. This began a cycle of slipping, getting back into recovery and then losing interest in going to meetings. The cycle continued to repeat.

Freeman tried to stop his behavior many times. But each effort ended when he had a slip or entered a period of full relapse. He even sought out the services of two therapists to help him deal with his compulsive sexual behavior but neither was experienced in treating sexual addiction. He even promised God that he would stop acting out. But none of these efforts provided him lasting relief from his addiction.

The fear of being caught led him to seek a therapist who specialized in sex addiction to help him stop his compulsive sexual behavior. With this solid reentry to recovery, he was finally able to establish long-term sobriety. He now has over five years of continuous sobriety. As part of his recovery program, Freeman continues to attend three 12-step meetings a week, he is currently sponsoring several other men, and he has one individual therapy session a month for added accountability.

Are slips and relapse inevitable?

No! While a large portion of the people entering recovery programs suffer setbacks or relapse, there are addicts in recovery who never slip or relapse. There should be expectancy for no slips or relapses. If individuals believe they are likely to slip, they may set up a self-fulfilling prophecy.

Slips are significant events in recovery that call for immediate attention. Often slips happen when the addict was not prepared. Slips result from repeated excursions into behaviors the sexual addict has identified as problematic. Someone said, S.L.I.P. means "sexual sobriety lost its priority." A slip or a relapse is a wake-up call that something must change.

What is the difference between a slip and a relapse?

A slip is a one-time event that happens unexpectedly and without planning. A relapse is a prolonged move back to compulsive sexual behavior. For example, a person spending the night acting out with a partner did not experience a slip, this is a relapse. And a person who has "slipped" and gone to an adult bookstore two weekends in a row has also experienced a relapse.

If one has a slip or a relapse, he must make immediate and often drastic changes to prevent the problem behavior from recurring. If the individual does not change anything, he can expect the destructive behavior to repeat. It is important that the sexual addict take immediate steps to return to solid recovery and help prevent further relapse.

Most in recovery from addictions experience missteps. Some clinical professionals teach that recovering persons should expect slips and perhaps relapse. Most sexual addicts try numerous things to stop their compulsive behavior before they get into solid recovery. Many of these attempts at sobriety were tried before anyone else knew about their addiction.

Once people have been confronted with undeniable proof of their addiction they may finally have the needed motivation to go all the way into recovery. The expectation that I give clients is that they should not have a single slip after this point. Slips may be common in 12-step circles, but that does not mean that a person in recovery should lessen his or her resolve to live in sobriety or that a slip is inevitable.

Slipped! Now What?

What do you do if your partner has a slip or a relapse? They must take steps to immediately return to solid recovery.

Levels of Care (LOC) of Treatment

Getting back into recovery may be different for each person. It depends if the person experienced a slip or a relapse as well as the behaviors. For a relapse, it is important to consider the length of time the person reengaged the addiction.

The following five Levels of Care are useful to help a person recover from a slip or relapse. The Level of Care that is necessary depends on the behavior and resolve of the sexual addict to make recovery a priority. The choice is to select a Level of Care that adequately addresses the problem and is the least intrusive. For example, a slip involving only masturbation may call for using LOC 2. A relapse with a return to acting-out behaviors will call for LOC 3.

Level of Care One (LOC 1)

LOC 1 is the basic level of care for clients entering therapy. It involves weekly individual therapy sessions. Clients are expected to attend 12-step meetings at least twice per week. After the client is stabilized and has gained a good foundation in recovery he is encouraged to begin group therapy as an adjunct to individual therapy.

Level of Care Two (LOC 2)

This involves an increase in 12-step meetings and therapy. The person should begin or restart therapy. A combination of individual therapy and, after a person has established a good recovery foundation, participation in group therapy is used. Following a slip or a relapse, the addict should have therapy twice a week. Some may benefit from therapy once a day for several weeks. If the client is not in group therapy, he should join a group as soon as possible. The increased therapy schedule should continue for three or more weeks, depending how the client responds. Therapy should be with a clinician who has been specifically trained to deal with sexual addiction.

LOC 2 requires attendance at three 12-step meetings each week and, if time and schedule allows increasing the number of meetings to more than three.

For some it is helpful to increase 12-step meeting attendance to one per day for ninety days (a 90/90). It may be difficult to find 12-step meetings that deal with sexual addiction every day of the week. This should not be seen as a reason to abandon doing a 90/90. Any 12-step meeting may supplement a sexual addict's regular meetings. When introducing him or herself at meetings, the recovering sexual addict can simply say, "I'm an addict from another fellowship." It is common for persons with various addictions to attend Alcoholic Anonymous meetings to augment their other recovery meetings. There are also online meetings for 12-step fellowships that a person can attend if he cannot find available meetings nearby.

It is important that sexual addicts contact their sponsor to insure they are aware of their slip and open to direction on how to reestablish the recovery program. If the addict does not have a sponsor, he must get one immediately. The lack of a sponsor may be a significant contributing factor for a slip.

Level of Care Three (LOC 3)

LOC 3 calls for a Three-Day Intensive focused on relapse recovery. These Intensives are tailored specifically to the needs of the individual who has slipped or relapsed. Actions and attitudes that may have contributed to the slip or relapse are reviewed by the therapist. Helping the client to reestablish a sustainable recovery routine is critical.

Three-Day Intensives are carefully coordinated with the client's home therapist, who also receives a discharge summary. Significant care is taken to ensure that the treatment provided will complement the continued therapy after the Intensive. The Intensive culminates with the client being led through the construction and implementation of a personal recovery plan. Relapse prevention is a focus of these Intensives. Most include an opportunity to take a polygraph exam to back up a disclosure.

There is an increase in 12-step meetings to a minimum of three meetings per week and perhaps including a 90/90. Attending these meetings should be seen as a priority for recovery. Unfortunately, there are some clients who view meetings as optional since there is no cost associated. It is not surprising there is a slip when a client has stopped attending recovery meetings on a regular basis.

Level of Care Four (LOC 4)

LOC 4 involves intensive out-patient treatment for one to three weeks or more. There are excellent agencies that provide this type of care, and can be found in the appendices section of this book. These intensives are designed to help a client reestablish recovery routines and prevent further relapses.

There should be an increase in attendance at 12-step meetings to a minimum of three meetings per week up to perhaps attending 90 meetings in 90 days. Meeting attendance alone will not impart recovery. The experience and hope shared at these meetings become the cornerstones of continued recovery.

Level of Care Five (LOC 5)

LOC 5 is the most demanding and extensive level of care. It includes in-patient treatment at a specialized facility for four to six weeks. This Level of Care disrupts daily life and may have significant impact on a job or career. However, as disruptive as inpatient treatment is, if a person does not respond to other Levels of Care, inpatient treatment may be the best option.

This Level of Care 5 is especially useful for clients who have multiple addictions. Common co-occurring addictions include alcohol and drug abuse, gambling addiction, and eating disorders. Treatment centers provide the best opportunity for dealing with multiple addictions together, which is imperative for successful recovery.

Inpatient treatment, as with all treatments, is dependent on the willingness of the sexual addict to be personally involved in his treatment. Treatment for sexual addiction is not a passive activity. It requires the addict to work, listen, learn, follow, and ultimately surrender to the treatment process. There are excellent facilities that provide this type of care (see Appendix A). An integral part of inpatient treatment is attending 12-step meetings. Some facilities include mandatory attendance to 12-step meetings. After treatment, the client should attend at least three meetings a week for six months and thereafter not less than two meetings per week. Some have a goal to attend 90 meetings in the first 90 days after discharge.

For each Level of Care, it is important for the sexual addict to examine his total recovery plan and identify deficits. Typical deficits are not making meetings a priority, not meeting with a sponsor, or not having contact with his Circle of Five. There may also be an absence of other recovery routines that support recovery or recovery-related reading. An examination of the recovering addict's life will likely show he had been engaging questionable behaviors for a time prior to the slip or relapse. To sum up:

LOC 1:
- One individual therapy session per week
- Two 12-step meetings per week.

LOC 2:
- Two individual therapy sessions per week. Some clients may require more therapy, up to one session each day.
- Attending a minimum of three 12-step meetings a week and consider starting a 90/90: attending 90 12-step meetings in 90 days.
- Increased therapy schedule should continue for three to six weeks or more depending on how the client responds.

LOC 3:
- Three-Day Relapse Recovery Intensive, The intensive should include a polygraph exam
- Attending a minimum of three 12-step meetings a week and consider starting a 90/90.
- Minimum of three 12-step meeting per week or consider a 90/90.

LOC 4:
- Intensive out-patient treatment for two to six weeks
- Minimum of three 12-step meeting per week or consider a 90/90.

LOC 5:

- In-patient treatment at a specialized facility for four to six weeks
- Minimum of three 12-step meetings per week for six months (may also consider a 90/90) and then never fewer than two meetings per week.

Consequences of a slip or relapse

Orville's Story

Orville's acting-out behavior had been limited to viewing Internet pornography and compulsive masturbation. Rather than minimize his addiction, Orville worked hard in recovery attending several meetings each week, meeting with his sponsor and having a weekly therapy session.

After three years of recovery from sexual addiction, Orville was feeling good about his recovery. Since he was sure he was doing well, he stopped attending 12-step meetings and quit meeting with his sponsor. He was certain that he would not act out again. Orville was certain that he was cured and he was confident that he would not go back to his old behavior.

He withdrew $50,000 from his retirement account for a remodeling project on his house. Soon after making the withdrawal he found the project was going to be delayed. He kept the money in a separate account so it would not be spent. But when his wife went out of town for a few days, he decided to call an escort service and agreed to pay the person $500 for a "date."

Over the next several weeks, Orville gradually acquired the habit of paying for sex until he was acting out every week. He liked the idea of sleeping with what he considered to be high-class women who demanded a thousand dollars or more. He did not keep track of the money he spent because he thought he could replace it before it was missed. However, as a surprise, his wife agreed to move ahead with the remodeling project and needed the money to pay the contractor. She discovered that the entire $50,000 had been spent.

Of even greater concern was the fact that he had withdrawn an additional $50,000 and had already spent most of it. She told Orville to move out of the house and filed for divorce.

If there is a relapse, seek immediate help to return to recovery. It is important to consider the consequences of relapse. An option is divorce; however, I encourage partners to consider postponing it. If a divorce is the best option, postpone it rather than putting an immediate end to the marriage because other steps may be taken to redeem the addict and save the marriage.

If the partner chooses not to divorce, boundaries must be made clear to the addict. The addict must know the partner could initiate divorce any time. The partner should communicate the gravity of the situation to the addict by taking explicit steps to respond to the consequences of acting out. This type of response does not mean that the partner is punishing the addict for being "bad." It means that any acting-out behavior has consequences.

Consequences for slips or relapse are additional expense of treatment and restrictions from renewed vigilance in recovery. Treatment is not meant to be a punishment. It is a consequence of acting out. Financial setbacks to the family brought on by a slip or a relapse should impact the addict the most.

This may mean that following a slip or a relapse, an addict needs to forgo recreational pursuits and restrict personal expenditures. For men, it may mean selling a boat or selling a luxury car and purchasing a used vehicle that is the minimum necessary to guarantee him transportation. For women, it may mean doing without beauty treatments and postponing wardrobe additions.

Another significant consequence may be for the addict to sign a post-nuptial agreement which would state that if the marriage ends from any future acting out, the addict will walk away from the marriage with less of the accumulated assets from the relationship. Executing a legal document with a bad behavior clause is a radical step. But if the marriage is to continue after a relapse, the partner needs to know that the addict is serious about staying in recovery.

If the partner accepts the sexual addict without any consequences, what will motivate a change? The addict might believe he can continue acting out and merely appear sorry if caught again. Thus, it is essential for the partner to set boundaries that have consequences from relapse.

One way of setting boundaries and outlining consequences is for the partner to determine what his response will be if the addict has a slip or a relapse. Rather than communicate these now, which may result in the addict being less committed to recovery the partner may want to outline them in a letter that is signed, dated, sealed, and placed in a secure location if it is needed in the future.

Chapter 12

A Blueprint for Rebuilding Broken Trust

When a couple first determines they are going to share a relationship, they give spontaneously and extend and receive trust. The exchange of trust is not earned but is a reciprocal commitment that takes place when two people fall in love. This has sometimes been referred to as a "trust bank." The bank is relatively full as the relationship develops. Deposits are continually made into the trust bank that helps to strengthen and add value to the relationship.

When trust is breached, relationships are shaken to their core. The trust bank is quickly drained and ends up becoming overdrawn. If there is no reason for trust, what is reason is there to continue loving? Some find that love and trust are so intertwined that they find it difficult to separate the two.

Trust is slowly rebuilt over time. There is an understandable impatience on the part of sexual addicts in recovery when their spouse or partner does not show trust after weeks or months of recovery. The man will frequently ask, "Doesn't she realize I am doing good recovery work?" Or in her case, "When is he going to trust me again?"

Trust can be rebuilt when there is reason to trust your partner again. It is understandable not to trust that person until you see evidence of solid recovery. Do not be trapped into believing that you must squelch your misgivings and suspicions because your partner says, "You have to believe me. I'm not acting out anymore!" You want to believe the recovering sexual addict you love, but remember the past lies and broken promises.

Disclosure and a successful polygraph do not necessarily rebuild trust. However, a truthful disclosure may reinvest "currency" in the trust bank. Much more must be done to rebuild trust. The honesty during a disclosure can lay the foundation.

I sometimes tell couples that truth telling during a disclosure and a successful polygraph patch the hole in the trust bucket. But the bucket is still empty. They can begin making deposits and hopefully trust will eventually be fully restored.

How do you rebuild trust?
Believe what you see. If your partner is doing the work of recovery and you see continued evidences of recovery, perhaps there is reason to begin to have trust again. While it is not healthy for you to be in the role of checking on your partner like a detective, you will see evidence that he is or is not worthy of trust.

Believe in your feelings. Unfortunately, many spouses have learned not to trust their feelings because the partner was so convincing in the past. They may have gone to extraordinary lengths to persuade you not to trust your feelings. Part of taking care of yourself is realizing that you can trust your feelings.

This is not to say that every time you feel suspicious that your partner is acting out. But in the past you denied suspicions and dismissed nagging feelings that something was going on behind your back. You convinced yourself it was all in your mind or your partner convinced you to trust his version of the truth and not your own.

You now have reason to be suspicious of behavior that does not fit your partner's normal behavior. When you see changes in his or her work schedule, spending habits or any area that causes you to wonder what else might be going on, you have a right to answers.

If suspicions are unfounded you can let go of your uneasiness. If later you have questions about the behavior, you have a right to know if your partner is continuing in recovery or is returning to addiction. As you find your partner keeping commitments, continuing meetings with a therapist and sponsor, attending 12-step meetings, and being trustworthy, you can slowly begin trusting your partner.

Never again will you trust him just because of love or because your partner is convincing. You will find that you can trust your partner's actions with what you can verify. Trust can return and be stronger than before, because you have a concrete basis for it.

When Ronald Reagan was president, his signature phrase for relations with the former Soviet Union was "trust but verify." What makes sense in negotiations between countries also makes sense as you seek to rebuild your relationship: trust but verify. Rely on what you can see. Believe what you know to be true. Have confidence in your partner's recovery when you see the evidence of recovery work. As trust returns, you will cease doubting your partner if he calls to apologize for working late. Your trust will no longer be predicated on your partner sounding believable, but because your partner is proving daily to be trustworthy.

Following disclosure, it is important to set up a process to keep the relationship free of secrets and provide an atmosphere in which trust can be rebuilt. There are two tools that help accomplish this. The first is a weekly check-in that the recovering sexual addict does with his or her partner called the FASTT Check-In. The second is to set a schedule of polygraph exams. The work done in recovery to this point has succeeded in halting the depletion of the "trust bank." Now you are investing in your account, which takes time. Be patient and concentrate to stay in solid recovery.

FASTT Check-In: Weekly Check-In With Partner

A FASTT Check-In is a brief weekly period where the addict gives his partner a progress report concerning recovery. The purpose of the FASTT Check-In is to keep the partner informed about the addict's recovery activities, normalize talking about recovery-related topics, and allow both partners to be alert for signs that recovery needs to receive greater priority. FASTT check-ins should continue for two years following disclosure, or if there has been a breech in sobriety, until two years of sobriety have been established. Check-ins are ongoing during this period and *are the responsibility of the sexual addict to initiate*. Most check-ins can be done in ten minutes or less. If there is a slip involved or there has been evasive behavior, the check-in may require additional time.

The couple needs to set the day and time for the check-in. A good time for the check-ins is an evening when both partners can engage in recovery work. For example, an excellent time would be when the husband and the wife both attend a 12-step meeting or at the end of a day when both have an individual therapy session. Once agreed to the schedule, there should be a commitment from both partners to make this a standing appointment. If one is traveling, the appointment should be kept by phone. The FASTT format should be followed for each check-in. F.A.S.T.T. stands for: 1. Feelings, 2. Activities in Recovery, 3. Sobriety Statement or Slip Report, 4. Threats, and 5. Tools.

1. Feelings Check

The check-in begins with the sexual addict talking about his current feelings. If multiple feelings are present, the sexual addict should try to get in touch with each, stating them to the partner. Feelings checks are especially important for men because often they relegate their feelings to a few such as mad, happy, or sad.

Some men have grown up with the understanding that "real men" do not show a range of feelings. They may have been shamed by a parent or a peer for displays of emotions not considered manly. As a result, they may need practice how to express their feelings and letting their partner know what they are experiencing.

This is particularly true when experiencing fear or shame. These feelings may seem very inappropriate to him. The weekly feelings check-in procedure helps get in touch with what is going on inside.

2. Activities in Recovery

Here the recovering sexual addict has the opportunity to talk about all recovery activities completed that week. If the individual is actively working on recovery, the list will be extensive. Some activities that will be included are therapy sessions, both individual and group, as well as attendance at 12-step meetings. While the recovering sexual addict cannot talk about the work that others do in 12-step meetings, he can tell the partner about attending meetings, discussions at the meeting, and what he shared.

While a detailed list of recovery activities provides the partner some comfort, it is important for the addict to recognize that this list is not meant to impress the partner but rather to be a compilation of the weeks' recovery activities. Recovery is both a state of mind and set of actions. Though the addict may say he is in a recovery state of mind, the partner has no way to validate it. However, a recitation of the sexual addict's regular recovery activities lends credence to the assertion the addict is in a state of recovery.

Another category of recovery-related activities involves accountability to others. Early in recovery, the recovering sexual addict should be meeting weekly with a sponsor. During meetings the sponsor gets a report how the sexual addict has progressed during the week as well as a chance to review given assignments.

The sponsor's job is to lead the addict through the 12 steps of recovery, which can take from several months to two years or more. During this time there are frequent reading and writing assignments. The sexual addict should be able to give a detailed report on the work done with the sponsor. It is important for the recovering addict to be able to do assignments in private, but not in secret. He needs to work on the assignments the sponsor gives without having to reveal the specific contents of what he writes.

This may seem as if it counters the desire to put secrets to an end, but it does not. Secrets must end but everyone has a right to some privacy. For example, when a person closes enters a bathroom, they are not asking for secrecy but rather for privacy. Recovery work requires a sexual addict to delve into the long-hidden dark recesses of memory.

In the same way, the sexual addict should be allowed to participate in therapy and maintain privacy about what takes place in there. The exercises she is involved in, the things talked about, and the journal entries made should be kept private as the recovering sexual addict completes the process. Privacy around the 12-step work and therapy are crucial for recovery.

Not only is the sexual addict accountable to a particular sponsor, but should also have other persons to whom he is accountable. One of these might be an accountability partner from a church or synagogue. This individual should be someone who knows the recovering sexual addict well and with whom he can share the challenges of addiction as well as the journey to recovery. An accountability partner should ask tough questions that get to the heart of how the sexual addict is living his life.

During the check-in with the partner, the sexual addict should be able to talk about various contacts with persons who hold him accountable, such as a Circle of Five or Sponsor. The contacts with these entrusted people will keep recovery a priority.

Another recovery activity is reading recovery-related books and literature. Most 12-step fellowships provide a publication that explains their recovery program as well as offering stories about people who have followed their program. There are many books about sexual addiction recovery that may be part of weekly reading. In addition to the great number of written materials on sexual addiction recovery, 12-step fellowships publish helpful recovery literature. Sustained recovery includes reading recovery-related weekly. Many recovering sexual addicts keep a recovery book on their night stand to read each evening.

3. Sexual Sobriety Statement or Slip Report

The next part of the check-in is the slip report, in which the sexual addict gives a statement about his sobriety. The sobriety statement includes the date of sobriety as well as the fact that the addict has been sober since the last check-in. For example, the individual might say, "I have been sober from all acting-out behaviors for the past week. And I have had continuous sobriety since February 7th of last year."

A slip *of any kind*, is reported. This "slip report" will include any behavior that would be considered unsound. For example, if a man has not acted out but recognized being a bit too friendly with someone from work, this will be revealed at this time. If a woman realized that her conversation with someone at the club was flirtatious, she would reveal this as part of the check-in. Regardless of how seemingly innocent the behavior, if there is the realization there was potential to act out, it is reported.

Some people protest sharing such things with their partners. They reason that they have not acted out or that their behavior has not been that out of line. However, the consequences of not revealing this behavior are significant. If he or she does not reveal this behavior then the recovering addict is starting to keep secrets. It cannot be overstressed that secrets have shame attached to them. The presence of secrets and shame allow the addiction to regain a foothold.

4. Threats

The word "trigger" for this part of the check-in was formerly used because it accurately describes what the sexual addict often faces. Sex Addicts Anonymous (the "Green Book") of Sex Addicts defines triggers as, "Any situation or behavior that causes us to feel a powerful desire to act out" (p. 68).

However, using the word "trigger" in the check-in often communicates to the partner that the presence of a trigger means that acting out is eminent. Experiencing triggers is a normal part of recovery. Their presence does not mean that an addict is teetering on the brink of losing sexual sobriety.

To better communicate what the addict faces daily, I use the word "threat" to describe situations that require recovery tools. Threats are a part of daily life for everyone. For example, staying in the sun too long presents the threat of developing skin cancer. Every time we get into an automobile, we should scan for conditions that could be a threat to safety and watch for threats from other drivers.

Sexual addicts should get in the habit of continually doing a threat assessment to guard against things that endanger their recovery. Threats are normal. They may be visual as well as emotional. There are also threats because of job stress or life crisis. During check-in, the addict should feel free to talk openly about every threat he encounters. If fact, if threats are seldom shared during a check-in, it would be safe to assume that the reason for the silence was not that there were no threats, but that they did not feel the threats could be shared. The more the check-in time becomes routine, the freer the sexual addict will be to share his threats.

5. Tools

If threats were shared and the check-in ended at that point, the partner would be concerned. After the threats are shared, the addict should discuss what tools were used to respond to each threat. A good practice is to share one trigger and to discuss what methods were used to address that threat.

Throughout recovery, sexual addicts learn a variety of effective methods to response to threats. Some of these tools are learned in therapy and 12-step groups. The tools may be as simple as breaking visual contact, followed by a making a vow of renewed sexual sobriety. Other tools may involve changing one's schedule to allow the individual to go to additional 12-step meetings. He may call a sponsor or someone in recovery for immediate support, or schedule an extra therapy session to process the threatening event as well as to prepare for handing similar future situations.

Additional Items

The check-in may include other items mutually agreed upon, such as accountability for time and money or a safety plan for travel. Any additional items that the couple wishes to include are their option.

As a minimum, the five points of the FASTT check in should be followed.

Some individuals choose later to do a check-in with their addicted partners. They check in about the recovery work they are doing for codependent behaviors. For the first year of check-ins, I recommend that only the sexual addict do the check-in. It is important to keep focus that the check-ins take place because of their sexual addiction and the damage done to the relationship.

Partner's Response

The partner's response to the check-in is crucial for success. Her role is to provide a safe place for the recovering sexual addict to talk about recovery. To accomplish this, the partner needs to do some things that may not initially feel natural.

During a check-in and for that evening, it is important for the partner not to ask questions about what is shared during the check-in. She will have time to ask questions later. The partner's role is to listen and provide a safe place to share and show appreciation for the check-in, and give a big hug when it is completed.

It is natural for a partner, who hears a particular visual threat to say, "You mean *that* was a threat to you! I don't understand." Men and women are threatened in different ways. A significant source of triggers for men are visual stimuli. A wife does not need to understand why her husband was threatened. She needs to accept the fact that he was threatened. It must be emphasized that a recovering sexual addict is not trying to shock his partner, but to confront the addiction through disclosure.

The next morning, if the partner wants additional details about something shared at the check-in, she may ask for details. The tone of questioning as well as the attitude during this process impacts how safe the addict feels about check-in the following week.

Follow-Up Polygraph Exams

Another important tool for keeping secrets at bay is to have follow-up polygraphs. These are similar to the baseline polygraph but the questions are designed to learn how well the sexual addict is doing in recovery. There is no attempt to gather further information predating the baseline polygraph.

It is important to give continued attention to recovery after the initial program with a rigorous aftercare program. After that, we encourage clients to have additional Aftercare Intensives every six months and up to three years after start of recovery. Annual One-day intensive aftercare sessions are recommended.

Addiction, according to the big book of Alcoholics Anonymous is, "Cunning, baffling, and powerful." Sex addiction is no exception. Even when recovery is going well, there may be a subtle temptation to act out. The knowledge that a polygraph is scheduled restores sanity long enough for a sexual addict to be able to break free from the power of the addiction and make choices consistent with good recovery. The polygraph exam is a great tool for recovery, because the sexual addict can use it for encouragement to do solid recovery work. It is also a most useful tool to help the individual become a person of integrity in every area of personal and professional life. This is especially true regarding being truthful in both actions and speech.

A benefit of follow-up polygraph exams is restored trust in the relationship. Rather than having to rely solely on a promise, the partner has proof that the addict has remained in recovery.

It is not enough to know that the addict is in recovery and all previous acting-out behavior has been revealed. What matters is gaining the truth at the beginning of recovery. If acting out continues, how can you know without a polygraph exam?

There may be initial reluctance or resistance on the part of couples to use on-going polygraph exams. Some protest that they should have trust without them. However, once trust is breached, what is the basis to restore it? Experience shows that trust without proof is not advisable.

Some say that polygraph exams used this way are a crutch and an effort should be made as soon as possible to get rid of the crutch. The exams may be a crutch. If a person needs a crutch to walk, why not use it? Is that not preferable to falling?

Rather than seeing polygraph exams as a crutch, they should be viewed as tools. They are effective to rebuild trust in a relationship. They deliver inestimable value to learn new thought and behaviors to replace the dysfunctional ones acquired in sexual addiction.

Scheduling a follow-up polygraph exam is the responsibility of the addict. The partner should not have to remind the addict that a polygraph exam is due, just as is not the job of the therapist to make sure that the recovering addict knows when an exam needs to be scheduled.

Follow-up polygraph exams are good occasions for celebration. By the time a couple is at this point in recovery, it is a virtual certainty that the exam will be passed. The celebration is for achieving another recovery milestone.

Success in recovery depends on sexual addicts taking responsibility for their own recovery. If they succeed in recovery it is because they have taken the steps necessary for their success. If they fail, they cannot blame their partners, therapists, or sponsors.

It cannot be stated more clearly: the sexual addict is the only one who can succeed at the work of recovery. He alone honors the hope and achieves the freedom from sexual addiction.

Chapter 13

When Is It Time To Move On?

Felix's Story

Felix was a good man. This was not just his evaluation of himself but also of Connie, his wife of 27 years. He entered recovery 12 years ago. During those years he had experienced what he considered a slip about every three months. Each time, he convinced Connie to take another chance on him as he recommitted to make recovery higher priority.

Felix always considered himself a bit shy. He had not dated much as a teenager. His wife was the first person he had ever kissed. He kept his various compulsive sexual behaviors carefully hidden from her. Every two or three days, Felix would visit a pornography site where he was a member to watch the latest videos.

His favorite videos were those categorized as "barely legal"—videos of teenage girls who were at least 18 years old but appeared to be younger. Next he would spend some time in adult chat rooms, again looking for older teenage girls willing to talk dirty to him. Felix found it easier to speak to teens.

On one occasion Felix was intrigued by an instant message from a girl who said, "I'm 15 but I look like I'm 25." He carried on a conversation with her over a period of six weeks. Several times she invited him to meet her in person but he initially declined. Eventually, he agreed to meet her at a shopping center, and was arrested when he stepped into the store. The girl was actually a federal agent posing as a juvenile to try to apprehend child predators who prey on children.

Felix is serving a sentence in a federal prison for solicitation of a minor, and is now registered as a sex offender.

It is common during the addiction and in recovery when spouses or partners wonder if it is time to end the relationship. This deserves additional attention. It is tragic that many marriages are destroyed because of sexual addiction. However, the discovery of compulsive sexual behavior need not mark the end to a relationship, even if that activity has involved other people and perhaps many. If the sexual addict is willing to get help and address the problem, the relationship can be saved and can thrive in recovery.

Some individuals have the mistaken belief that if their spouse or partner has been unfaithful that they must get a divorce. Unfaithfulness is devastating, and spouses believe the acting out will occur again, and again. Rather than look for a way out, couples can look for way to stay in relationships and put the pieces back together.

Addictions often develop over a lifetime. They are behaviors reinforced by years of acting out and powerful neurochemical highs. Recovery for many people is a series of starts and stops, and resolutions followed by relapses. Rather than seeing recovery as a steady uphill progression, it is more like a roller coaster with ups and downs, yet all the time moving forward.

If an individual is committed to a program of recovery, even if he is continuing to have setbacks, there is reason to hope that he may be able to get free from all compulsive behavior and live the rest of his or her life in sexual integrity. Do not lose hope!

When the Sexual Addict Refuses Help

What about relationships where sexual addicts are not willing to get help? If your partner admits to having a problem with compulsive sexual behavior but refuses to address that problem, it is time to consider ending the relationship.

Sometimes when a partner sets this boundary and the addict is convinced of the seriousness of the boundary, he may realize his only choice to save the relationship is to get help for his addiction.

I have numerous cases where divorce papers had been filed, only to stop to legal proceedings when the sexual addict decides to get help.

This does not suggest that threats of divorce or abandonment are to be used to manipulate sexual addicts into recovery. When a spouse reaches the point where she is getting ready to end the relationship, the decision is often enough to persuade the sexual addict to seek immediate help.

What about the cases where addicts continue to slip or relapse? This may also be the time to consider ending the relationship. If that happens, it is important to recognize that the addict's decision to put the addiction ahead of his partner resulted in forfeiting the relationship.

No one does recovery perfectly. Unfortunately, many have slips and relapses that punctuate their recovery. If steps are taken to rectify the situation and restore good recovery routines, the relationship is worth salvaging.

If the sexual addict is not willing to do the work of recovery, even after repeated opportunities to get help, it may be time to end the relationship. Moving on may mean leaving your spouse or partner trapped in his addiction. Therefore, your partner must accept that you will no longer allow yourself to be traumatized by continued acting out.

If this is the place you find yourself and you have given your partner repeated chances to get into recovery, but he refused or will not maintain a program of sobriety, then you may feel that he has chosen the addiction over you. Ending the relationship is a difficult decision and one that you should make only after much soul-searching and consulting with professionals and trusted friends. Life without your partner will be challenging and perhaps painful, but ask yourself, wouldn't that pain be less than remaining in the relationship if your partner's acting out never ended?

Often the sexual addict will do everything possible to save the relationship, when he realizes that the spouse is ready to end it. If the shock of the partner saying the relationship is over gets an addict into recovery, then he can be grateful that something was stronger than the power of addiction, and that was coming face-to-face with the loss of the relationship.

The relationship is over. What went wrong?

In some cases the relationship was over before the partner knew the extent of the spouse's addiction. Or the sexual addict announced that he had found someone who "really knows how to love me" and walked away from the relationship without trying to save it. Abrupt endings are devastating and leave lasting wounds.

Some individuals who are sexually addicted never get into recovery and continue to resist all offers of recovery. Their partners set boundaries, give ultimatums, make impassioned pleas, and otherwise beg their partners to get into recovery and give the relationship a chance. But they find that they are powerless over their partners' addictions and cannot bring them to recovery.

In other cases, recovery is not constant with some addicts and they continue to suffer slips and relapses. They make promises that they will stop their destructive behavior, but it never sticks. After a few sessions of therapy and 12-step meetings, they declare themselves "cured" and stop all recovery actions. The repeated relapses finally bring partners to the point of saying, "Enough!"

There are other relationships where the husband and the wife get into recovery but the relationship still does not work. For some cases there was too great of an imbalance in recovery; that is, one partner was well ahead of the other and the other never caught up. In some of these relationships, even though recovery appears to be going well for both, they cannot make the relationship work. The wounds of deceit are sometimes too deep to heal. In some cases, one or both partners are unable to move to a place of acceptance as a prelude to forgiveness so that healing can begin. There are some spouses hurt so much that they can never get to a place of healing.

It really does not matter what finally happened because the relationship is over. Wishing, hoping, crying, and pleading will not restore that which has been severed.

If your relationship has ended, here are a few things about your future that you need to hear:

First, don't date until you have continued further in your own recovery journey. You need time to make sense of your feelings and concentrate on yourself. No "rebound" relationship will provide the nurturing you now need. If you are dating, stop immediately. You deserve to have time to take care of yourself. Life is not going to pass you by while you are concentrating on giving yourself what you need.

Second, you need time to heal. If you are not in therapy at present, start therapy immediately. You will need to do some intensive family-of-origin work to work on childhood wounds that may be impacting your life today. This would also be a good time to find an EMDR therapist who can help you address your trauma issues.

It is especially important that you get professional help to determine the impact of the relationship with your former partner. You may be able to see some similarities in your former partner and other people with whom you have had relationships. In fact, some individuals are candid enough to admit that they seem to always end up with someone who is an addict or someone who is abusive to them. Addicts are often charming, persuasive, and focused on the person who is the object of their affection. If you have chosen an addict of any variety in any or perhaps every previous relationship, this would be a good time to ask yourself, "What do I need to do to heal, and quit living the same traumatic relationship repeatedly?"

If this is you, you alone can change the next chapter of your life. You are the author of your own future. No matter how long you have let others tell how to live your life, you are free now to assume control of the events in your life.

You deserve a healthy relationship. Do not settle for less.

This would also be a good time for you to cement relationships with other men or women who are healing from relationships that have damaged their self-esteem. Twelve-Step organizations are important sources of support to individuals who have found themselves alone after the end of a relationship to a sexual addict.

Even if there is not a 12-step group for partners in your area, Co-SA online groups can be very beneficial.

Chapter 14

Closing Message

Adventure in Recovery

In the course of their recovery journey, I tell my clients that they will be able to look at themselves in the mirror and say, "You are a good person," and know in their hearts that the words are true. Negative self-talk that has plagued them since childhood gradually end and will be replaced with healing words. I believe recovery is truly an adventure. In the end, sexual addicts have a much fuller, richer, more meaningful life than if they had not had compulsive behaviors to conquer.

Sexual addiction recovery can be an adventure. As with many adventures, recovering from sexual addiction never stops. It continues throughout life. Sexual addicts never get to the point where all of their recovery work is done. They continue to face new challenges and additional parts of their character upon which to focus. Yet as long as they are living free from compulsive behavior, their addiction is behind them. Their journey of freedom continues and never has to stop.

As you continue through the many tasks of recovery, you will find challenges and numerous blessings. As you and your partner take this journey together, you will have the opportunity to work on some things that would have escaped your notice if it were not for addiction and recovery.

In the Big Book of Alcoholics Anonymous, in the section referred to as "the promises," it states that there will come a time when a person will "not regret the past nor wish to shut the door on it."

While this seems unattainable, it becomes reality for many. Perhaps it is more fully realized when a couple takes the recovery journey together.

Certainly there are hurts and pains from the past that bring grief. There are things that recovering addicts regret. That regret is shared by their partners. Addiction wounds both the addicted and those who love them. It is a vicious circle that can only be severed by making a commitment to do the work necessary to end all compulsive behavior forever.

Recovery has many rewards. One is the ability to look back on a relationship that has grown in ways not thought possible. Being in relationship with a sexual addict has its down side, to be sure. But if the partner is doing solid recovery work and actively engaged in his or her own work, the relationship possesses a new dimension of richness that could not have come were it not for addiction and recovery.

The presence of sexual addiction in a relationship does not mean that a relationship must end. Nor does it mean that happiness must end. If both the addict and the partner are willing to address the addiction, work on their individual recoveries, and recover as a couple, there is every reason to hope for a good outcome for the relationship.

I am committed to counseling because I see miracles happen on a daily basis. I continually come meet individuals and couples who believe their happiness is at an end because of the compulsive sexual behavior. But relationships do not have to end.

I am constantly amazed at the changes that can take place in relationships through solid recovery work. I hear couples who have been in recovery several months state that their relationship is better now than it has ever been. I have heard that enough times that I have come to expect that result when both are committed to doing whatever it takes to restore their relationship.

My desire for you and your partner is that you immerse yourselves in recovery. I urge you to be willing to do the courageous and challenging work that is required. As a Frances Bacon once said, "All rising to a great place is by a winding stair."

May your recovery journey of hope lead you to freedom.

Appendix A

Recovery Programs at
Hope & Freedom Counseling Services

Wallace's Story

Wallace entered recovery after Karen discovered his acting out two years ago. He had done pretty well in recovery and attending a 12-step meeting each week and meeting with his sponsor. As far as Karen knew he had not acted out since entering recovery. She attended her own 12-step meetings to help her understand how she had missed the signs of her husband's acting out. She learned how to set boundaries as well as develop behaviors that helped her become more emotionally healthy in her recovery.

While their recoveries were going well, their relationship continued to suffer. Karen realized that she did not trust Wallace and not sure that she had the complete truth about his past acting-out behavior. They came to Hope & Freedom Counseling Services to rebuild their relationship and insure they each remained on track with their recovery by doing a Three-Day Intensive.

One of the treatment options we offer at Hope & Freedom Counseling Services is Three-Day Intensives. These are particularly good for individuals or couples first entering recovery. They are an ideal forum to deal with the crisis that may have precipitated recovery. Intensives are also good for anyone who have not been able to maintain long-term sobriety or experienced a slip or relapse.

Three-Day Intensives are short but concentrated periods to focus on a particular aspect of recovery. They are not a "Three-Day Cure." There is no such thing. Rather, it is to do intensive recovery work, to develop a good foundation for recovery or to address a specific need during recovery. Hope & Freedom Counseling Services offers a variety of Three-Day Intensives that are especially helpful for persons who live in geographical areas where sexual addiction therapy is not available.

These are not the treatment choice for every one or couple where compulsive sexual behavior is a factor. We accept fewer couples than apply for this treatment program. There are a number of factors that may not make this the treatment option of choice.

Persons considering a Three-Day Intensive must be willing to work hard. They must be prepared to do whatever is necessary to stop the destructive behaviors related to sexual addiction and be willing to take extraordinary steps to restore their relationship. For the intensive process to be successful, it requires couples to be willing to participate in the three-day experience, and also willing to work hard on rigorous assignments each evening. The intensives we offer work best for highly motivated clients.

A prerequisite for participating in an intensive is for both partners to be stable emotionally. Clients with untreated obsessive-compulsive disorder, bipolar disorder, or severe attention deficit hyperactivity disorder may not be good candidates for intensives. After these disorders are stabilized with medication and therapy, they may be ready for the rigorous intensive process. Additionally, persons in danger of harming themselves are not appropriate for intensives.

Couples who are approved for participation in Three-Day Intensives must make an unqualified commitment to stay in the relationship after the intensive. This is crucial since disclosures typically reveal additional acting-out behaviors or some details about them. This new information traumatizes the partner. When the pain associated with trauma starts, the typical response it to look to anything to stop the pain, including ending the relationship.

We ask partners to make a commitment to stay in the relationship for a minimum of 12 months after the intensive. We ask sexual addicts to double the commitment and to stay in the relationship a minimum of 24 months after the intensive, regardless of their partner's anger or disappointment. Couples must agree to enter a contractual agreement with that goal to participate in the Hope & Freedom Three-Day Intensive.

If there is significant resistance on the part of a couple or an individual, Three-Day Intensives are not indicated. We ask couples who come to intensives to be willing to devote total effort to recovery for the three days. That includes not conducting any "business as usual" during the intensive. We also ask that contacts with home and family be minimized for the duration of the intensive.

People interested in intensives must complete an online application and next need to be screened to make sure they are appropriate for an intensive and also that there is a reasonable expectation that they will benefit from it.

The intensive is customized to the specific needs of each client. The intensives are offered for couples as well as individually for men. However, if the client is in a committed relationship, we strongly urge that the couple attend the intensive together, because successful recovery depends on both partners being involved in the recovery process. (Information and applications about intensives may be found at www.HopeAndFreedom.com .) The following is a partial list of intensives offered through Hope & Freedom Counseling Services

Recovery Foundations Intensive

Recovery Foundations Intensives are designed for men and couples at the beginning of recovery and often focus to give participants a broad understanding of sexual addiction and what is involved in recovery. There is an emphasis on understanding the origins of addiction and the factors that contribute to sexual addiction.

These intensives focus to integrate recovery routines into the couples' relationship as well as reestablish trust in the relationship. Relapse prevention is a significant focus. The Recovery Foundations Intensive culminates with each client drafting a personal recovery plan.

Restoration Intensive for Couples or for Individuals

This intensive is structured for couples where the client has been in recovery a while but has had a slip or a relapse. Attention is given to understanding the cause of the relapse and preventing further relapses. A significant focus of this intensive is dealing with the issue of trust. The couple is introduced to a process of trust rebuilding that requires significant commitment from each. It offers a high success rate. A similar intensive is offered for individuals.

Survivors Intensive for Couples or for Individuals

This intensive is designed for couples where one or both partners have experienced significant past trauma. The trauma may to go back to childhood or be recent and resulted from current sexual acting out. This Intensive focuses on each partner doing significant healing around the trauma and also looking at the impact the trauma has on the relationship. A similar intensive is offered for individuals.

Step-Down Intensive for Couples or for Individuals

This intensive is designed as a step-down treatment for couples where the sexual addict has just returned from inpatient treatment or from an extended intensive outpatient treatment facility. The emphasis is on reentering public life. Clients learn to identify and deal with daily triggers as well as learn new thought and behavior patterns to replace dysfunctional thoughts and behaviors. Relapse prevention and developing a personal recovery plan round out the intensive.

Couples Communication Intensive

This intensive is open only to couples who have already done significant work in recovery or where sexual addiction is not a factor. For couples in recovery, prerequisites include a complete disclosure and the establishment of a period of unbroken sobriety. The material for this intensive draws heavily on the work of Pia Mellody and Terry Real. The participants learn to identify and set healthy boundaries around talking and listening and learn new relationship skills. There is an emphasis on learning to recognize strategies that cause a lose-lose situation in a relationship.

The culmination of the intensive is for the couple to develop a Fair Fight Contract and learn how to disagree without ending their relationship. Couples work through real-life issues and are taught to be in touch with their emotions and to support each other during disagreements. There is an emphasis to help both understand how family of origin issues may be contributing to their communication problems as a couple.

Special Topic Intensives

We offer special topic intensives designed to fit specific clients' needs. These deal with a number of topics related to recover; such as multiple addictions, couples where the husband and the wife have addictions, recovery issues involving the family, or religious abuse.

High Profile Client Intensive

Individuals in the public eye face special challenges entering recovery. If they go into a therapy office they risk revealing their struggle with compulsive sexual behavior. To address this concern, we take the Intensive to the client. This intensive is good for any high-profile person including senior executives, professional athletes, politicians, actors, broadcast personalities, and celebrities. These are offered at a discrete location in the United States or Canada. The content is customized to fit the needs of the individual or couple. The location is chosen that allows for an extra buffer of anonymity that is not available for celebrities who enter well-known treatment centers.

Additional intensives are offered to meet the special needs of physicians and clergy. These intensives are highly individualized to deal with the specific issues involved. In cases where an extra level of anonymity is needed, we offer intensives at locations other than our main site.

Super Intensives

Super Intensives are special purpose intensives offered to couples with long-standing difficulties that have not found resolution by any other means. Addiction may or may not be a factor. Super Intensives are also useful for treatment involving families or other special purposes. A limited number are offered each year. Only couples who have failed to resolve conflict and/or reestablish trust by more traditional types of psychotherapy are considered for Super Intensives.

Preparing for Intensives

Clients preparing for an intensive are encouraged to make adequate preparations to ensure the success of their concentrated work. They are encouraged to spend time thinking about the events that have contributed to the need for the intensive. For intensives dealing with sexual addiction, it is important to make a complete, detailed, but confidential list of all acting-out behaviors. The more detailed and complete this list, the more effective the intensive.

Clients who participate in a Three-Day Intensive are encouraged to take care of all business and family matters before coming to the intensive and not to conduct any business during the intensive. Frankly, we have found that clients who conduct "business as usual" during an intensive get limited benefit. For this reason, we strongly encourage clients to schedule an intensive when they are able to devote their full concentration to continuous therapy over three days.

To maximize the effectiveness of this time, we have the following stipulations:

- Leave cell phones, pagers, Blackberries, PDAs, iPods, laptops, and other electronic devices at home.
- Refrain from conducting business during the duration of the intensive.
- Limit phone calls to one per day to check with family or to check on dependent children.

- Do not drink any alcohol for the thirty days preceding the intensive.
- Refrain from all alcohol use during the intensive.
- Do not watch television during the intensive.

The total focus of the three days is to concentrate on individual recovery and strengthening the relationship. Distractions must be kept to a minimum. Nothing should be allowed to hinder the important work that takes place during an intensive.

It is beneficial for clients to stay an extra day or longer after the intensive to process with their partner what they have learned and accomplished during the preceding three days. This time can be important as couples make plans to reenter life and consider how their restored relationship may be different in the future.

Aftercare Intensives

A rigorous aftercare program is an important ingredient in any recovery treatment program. After the initial three days of work we encourage couples to come back for periodic One-Day Aftercare Intensives. These are mini versions of a Three-Day Intensive. During the Aftercare Intensives, couples have a combination of individual and couples therapy. The Aftercare Intensives are used to checkup on recovery progress, and for the couple to learn additional tools of recovery and work on communication issues they may be facing. A follow-up polygraph exam may be used to verify that acting out has not recurred.

The first of these one-day follow ups is scheduled three months after the Three-Day Intensive. They are scheduled every six months for an additional eighteen to thirty-six months depending on the couple's need. Thereafter we encourage couples to schedule an Aftercare Intensive annually as a checkup on the relationship and monitor progress in recovery.

Appendix B

Recovery Progress Chart & Inspirational Audio Messages

This Interactive Weekly Recovery chart helps to enhance positive steps needed to achieve hope & freedom.

Markers are made to indicate those places, days, or situations that addictive regression occurred.

If you adhere to the plan, noting the times you enhanced community with your partner, exercised to deal with stress, or followed through with a goal, you will find that the recovery chart will reinforce your behavior with more positive experiences.

Audio messages, each approximately 20 minutes in length, and narrated by Dr. Milton Magness in a professional yet relaxed and encouraging tone, dealing with the following areas:

1. Am I a Sex Addict?
2. Lost in Cyber Space
3. Intensive Preparation for Her
4. Intensive Preparation for Him
5. Getting Started in Recovery I
6. Getting Started in Recovery II
7. Disclosure
8. Accountability in Recovery

These audio messages are particularly beneficial when the sexual addict or partner could benefit from a caring, professional voice giving them reinforcement for the path they have taken to freedom from addiction. They are available at www.RecoveryOnTheGo.com

Weekly Recovery Record

		DAY	Monday	Tuesday
		Date:		
POSITIVE		**Exercise** (type)		
		Duration (minutes)		
		Diet Quality (junk to healthy)	1 2 3 4 5	1 2 3 4 5
		Amount (small to excessive)	1 2 3 4 5	1 2 3 4 5
		Sleep (hours)		
	Mental			
	Spiritual – Acknowledgment of God or the spiritual realm			
	Relationships – Affirmation with spouse/ partner			
	Friends – Contact/maintaining relationships			
	Communication – with spouse/partner			

Sunday – Most rewarding experience OR accomplishment of the week:

BEHAVIORS

KEY: T = Temptation **A** = Acting-out

NEGATIVE	Monday	Tuesday
Alcohol	T A	T A
Drugs	T A	T A
Cybersex	T A	T A
Pornography	T A	T A
Sexual Fantasy	T A	T A
Masturbation	T A	T A
Phone Sex	T A	T A
Escort Service/Massage Parlor	T A	T A
Prostitution	T A	T A

Sunday – Most difficult temptation during the week that you successfully overcame:

Wednesday	Thursday	Friday	Saturday	Sunday
1 2 3 4 5	1 2 3 4 5	1 2 3 4 5	1 2 3 4 5	1 2 3 4 5
1 2 3 4 5	1 2 3 4 5	1 2 3 4 5	1 2 3 4 5	1 2 3 4 5

T A	T A	T A	T A	T A
T A	T A	T A	T A	T A
T A	T A	T A	T A	T A
T A	T A	T A	T A	T A
T A	T A	T A	T A	T A
T A	T A	T A	T A	T A
T A	T A	T A	T A	T A
T A	T A	T A	T A	T A
T A	T A	T A	T A	T A

Resource Guide

Organizations Dedicated to Helping Sexual Addicts and their Partner

S-Anon
(615) 833-3152
www.sanon.org

Sex and Love Addicts Anonymous (SAA)
(210) 828-7900
www.slaafws.org

Sex Addicts Anonymous (SAA)
(713) 869-4902
www.sexaa.org

Sexual Addiction Resources/Dr. Patrick Carnes
www.sexhelp.com

Sexual Compulsives Anonymous (SCA)
(310) 859-5585
www.sca-recovery.org

Sexaholics Anonymous (SA)
(866) 424-8777
www.sa.org

Co-Dependents of Sex Addicts (Co-SA)
(763) 537-6904
www.COSA-recovery. org

Additional 12-Step Organizations

Adult Children of Alcoholics (AA)
(310) 534-1815
www.adultchildren.org

Al-Anon
(757) 563-1600
www.al-anon-alateen.org

Alateen (ages 12-17)
(757) 563-1600
www.al-anon-alateen.org

Alcoholics Anonymous
(212) 870-3400
www.aa.org

Co-Dependents Anonymous (Co-DA)
(602) 277-7991
www.codependents.org

Emotions Anonymous (EA)
(651) 647-9712
www.emotionsanonymous.org

Families Anonymous (FA)
(800) 736-9805
www.familiesanonymous.org

Gamblers Anonymous (GA)

(213) 386-8789

www.gamblersanonymous.org

Recovering Couples Anonymous

(781) 794-1456

www.recovering-couples.org

Bibliography

[1]*2006 Worldwide Pornography Revenues.* (2009). Retrieved August 4, 2009, from Top Ten Reviews: www.toptenreviews.com

[2]Lane, F. S. (2001). *Obscene Profits: The Entrepreneurs of Pornography in the Cyber Age.* New York: Routledge.

[3]Burke, G. (2009). *North America - United States - Christianity - Catholic.* Retrieved August 4, 2009, from WorldWide Religious News: www.uurn.org

[4]Taylor, R. (2009). *Sex-Trade Workers Trafficked Around the World.* Retrieved August 4, 2009, from suite101.com: http://human-rights-violations.suite101.com

[5]*Annual CDC Report Finds High Burden of Sexually Transmitted Diseases, Especially Among Women and Racial Minorities.* (2009). Retrieved August 4, 2009, from Centers for Disease Control and Prevention: www.cdc.gov

[6]*Populations Estimates.* (2008). Retrieved August 4, 2009, from U.S. Census Bureau: www.census.gov

[7]*Sexual Addiction.* Retrieved August 4, 2009, from Society for the Advancement of Sexual Health: www.sash.net

[8]*Internet Pornography Statistics.* Retrieved August 4, 2009, from Top Ten Reviews: www.internet-filter-review.toptenreviews.com

[9]Cooper, A. (2000). *Cybersex: The Dark Side of the Force.* Taylor Frances, p. 2.

[10]*Internet Pornography Statistics.* Retrieved August 4, 2009, from Top Ten Reviews: www.internet-filter-review.toptenreviews.com

[11]*Sex and Tech: Results from a Survey of Teens and Young Adults.* (2009). Retrieved August 4, 2009, from The National Campaign to Prevent Teen and Unplanned Pregnancy: www.thenationalcampaign.org

[12]*American Heritage Dictionary, Third Edition.* (1992). Boston: Houghton Mifflin.

[13]*Alcoholics Anonymous, Fourth Edition.* (2001). Alcoholics Anonymous, p. 58.

[14]Schneider, J., Corley, D., & Irons, R. (1998). Surviving Disclosure of Infidelity: Results of an International Survey of 164 Recovering Sex Addicts and Their partners. *Sexual Addiction & Compulsivity*, 189-217.

[15]Mellody, P. (1989). *Facing Codependence: What It Is, Where It Comes From, How It Sabotages Our Lives.* HarperCollins.

[16]Carnes, P. (2001). *Out of the Shadows: Starting Sexual and Relationship Recovery.* Center City: Hazelden

[17]Kubler-Ross, E. (1969). *On Death and Dying.* Touchstone

[18]Coop-Gordon, K., Baucom, D., & Snyder, D. (2004). An Intergrative Intervention for Promoting Recovery from Extra Marital Affairs. *Journal of Marital and Family Therapy,* p. 213.

[19]Steffens, B., & Rennie, R. (2006). The Traumatic Nature of Disclosure for Wives of Sexual Addicts. *Sexual Addiction and Compulsivity*, 247-267.

[20]*Eye Movement Desensitization and Reprocessing.* Retrieved August 4, 2009, from EMDR Institute, Inc.: www.emdr.com

Recommended Readings

Books

Alcoholics Anonymous
  by Anonymous

Sex and Love Addicts Anonymous
  by Anonymous

Out of the Shadows: Understanding Sexual Addiction
  by Patrick Carnes, Ph.D.

Don't Call it Love: Recovery from Sexual Addiction
  by Patrick Carnes, Ph.D.

The Betrayal Bond: Breaking Free of Exploitive Relationships
  by Patrick Carnes, Ph.D.

Mending a Shattered Heart
  edited by Stephanie Carnes, Ph.D.

A Woman's Way Through the Twelve Steps
  by Stephanie S. Covington, Ph.D.

Women, Sex, and Addiction: A Search for Love and Power
  by Charlotte S. Kasl, Ph.D.

Boundaries – Where You End And I Begin: How To Recognize and Set Healthy Boundaries
  by Anne Katherine, MA

Healing Together: A Guide to Intimacy and Recovery for
Co-Dependent Couples
　　by Wayne Kritsberg

Your Sexually Addicted Spouse: How Partners Can Cope and Heal
　　by Barbara Steffens, Ph.D. and Marsha Means, MA

Confronting Your Spouse's Pornography Problem
　　by Rory C. Reid, MSW and Dan Gray, LCSW

Rebuilding Trust: For Couples Committed to Recovery
　　by Jennifer Schneider, M.D. & Burt Schneider

Love Sick: One Woman's Journey through Sexual Addiction
　　by Sue William Silverman

Women Who Love Sex Addicts: Help for Healing from the Effects of a
Relationship With a Sex Addict
　　by Douglas Weiss & Donna DeBusk

Articles

Bancroft, J. , Vukadinovic, Z. (2004). Sexual Addiction, Sexual
　　Compulsivity, Sexual Impulsivity, or What? Toward a
　　Theoretical Model. *The Journal of Sex Research.* Aug 2004.
　　(41): 3-225.

Birchard, T. (2006) Addictions Without Substance Series, Part 1:
　　Sexual Addiction. *Drugs and Alcohol Today.* Jul 2006. (6): 2-32.

Cooper, A. The Dark Side of the Force, Cooper, A. (1998). Sexuality
　　and the Internet: Surfing into the new millennium. *Cyber*
　　Psychology and Behavior, I, 187-194.

Cooper, A, Delmonico, D., & Burg, R. (2000). Cybersex users,
　　abusers, and compulsives: New findings and implications.
　　Sexual Addiction and Compulsivity, (7): 1-2, 5-29.

Cooper, A., Scherer, C., Boies, S., & Gordon, B. (1999). Sexuality on the Internet: From sexual exploration to pathological expression. *Professional Psychology: Research and Practice,* (30) 154.

Delmonico, D., & Carnes, P. (1999). Virtual sex addiction: When cybersex becomes the drug of choice. *Cyber Psychology and Behavior,* (2) 457-463.

Griffiths, M. (2001). Sex on the Internet: Observations and implications for Internet sex addiction. *Journal of Sex Research,* (38) 333-342.

About the Author

Milton S. Magness, D.Min., is the founder and director of Hope & Freedom Counseling Services in Houston. He is a Certified Sex Addiction Therapist (CSAT) and a Licensed Professional Counselor.

Dr. Magness in on the board of directors of The Society for the Advancement of Sexual Health (SASH), formerly known as the National Council on Sex Addiction and Compulsivity, serving as the President of the board of that organization. He studied with Dr. Patrick Carnes, the foremost authority on sexual addiction, and has completed specialized study in the area of cybersex addiction. Dr. Magness has led national workshops on cybersex addiction and has conducted a multi-state research study that focused on cybersex behavior and recovery among self-identified sex addicts. He is a frequent speaker at both professional and public events.

Should you wish to contact Dr. Magness with questions about this book or for information on Hope & Freedom Counseling, you may write to him at milton.magness@hopeandfreedom.com or contact by telephone at (713) 630-0111.

Dr. Magness lives in Houston, Texas and Canmore, Alberta, Canada.